WHY POETRY

also by matthew zapruder

AMERICAN LINDEN (2002)

THE PAJAMAIST (2006)

SECRET WEAPON: SELECTED LATE POEMS OF EUGEN
JEBELEANU (TRANS., WITH RADU IOANID, 2008)

COME ON ALL YOU GHOSTS (2010)

SUN BEAR (2014)

why poetry

MATTHEW ZAPRUDER

ecce

An Imprint of HarperCollins*Publishers*

WHY POETRY. Copyright © 2017 by Matthew Zapruder. All rights reserved. Printed in the United States of America. No part of this book may be used or reproduced in any manner whatsoever without written permission except in the case of brief quotations embodied in critical articles and reviews. For information, address HarperCollins Publishers, 195 Broadway, New York, NY 10007.

HarperCollins books may be purchased for educational, business, or sales promotional use. For information, please email the Special Markets Department at SPsales@harpercollins.com.

FIRST EDITION

Designed by Renata De Oliveira

Library of Congress Cataloging-in-Publication Data has been applied for.

ISBN 978-0-06-234307-9

17 18 19 20 21   LSC   10 9 8 7 6 5 4

FOR MY FATHER

and for Sarah and Simon

Stop this day and night with me and you
shall possess the origin of all poems . . .
                    —WALT WHITMAN

Extreme clarity is a mystery.
                    —MAHMOUD DARWISH

The poet is always our contemporary.
                    —VIRGINIA WOOLF

contents

introduction

"I HAVE A CONFESSION TO MAKE: I DON'T REALLY UNDERSTAND poetry." For over twenty-five years, I have heard this said, over and over in slightly different ways, by friends, family, colleagues, strangers I met in bars and at dinner parties, on planes—so many people, practically everyone who found out I was a poet. Clearly, there is something about poetry that rattles and mystifies people, that puts them off, that makes them feel as if there is something wrong. Maybe the problem is with them as readers. Maybe they don't know enough or haven't studied enough or weren't paying attention in school. Or maybe the problem is with poetry itself. Why don't poets just say what they mean? Why do they make it so hard?

Around ten years ago, I had published two books of poetry and was traveling extensively around the United States and parts of Europe giving readings. I was also teaching poetry at a variety of colleges and universities, to a wide range of students. I kept hearing some version of that confession. And I kept having the same sorts of conversations, in which I would attempt to explain, stumblingly, what I believed about poetry, how I thought it made meaning, why I thought it was not difficult in the ways that we had been taught in school.

Later, I would each time always wish I had said it all differently, more gracefully, more completely. So, I thought, I will write a book. In it, I would explore what it is about poetry that makes people feel that they don't understand it. I would take seriously the objections people have, and try to address those objections clearly and simply, in order to explore what poetry is, and why, despite its supposed difficulties and obscurities, so many people still write and read it.

I was immediately excited about this big, impossible plan. I knew the main idea would be that poetry does something different than all other forms of writing and speech, something essential, something we need.

I would demonstrate this by writing about old poems, and also contemporary ones. I would discuss the mechanisms of poems: form, and rhyme, and metaphor, and symbols. I would reveal that what is strange about poetry—its dream logic, its interest in the slipperiness and material qualities of language, its associative daydreaming movement—is not some deliberate obfuscation, or an obstacle to communication, but essential to the very way poetry makes meaning.

Also, I would write about how the increasing pervasiveness of connective technology has made the contemplative, speculative, drifting yet attentive awareness poetry can bring ever more rare and necessary. I would write about how poetry can move us closer to what is vital and elusive, what can never be fully explained. I would write about contradiction, about Keats's formulation of negative capability, about Lorca's *duende,* and about the utopian dreams of the Surrealist poets. I would write about the excellence of dictionaries, and the necessity of getting literal with language, and how the slippery, provisional nature of language itself is intimately related to the power of poetry. I would also not leave out the way poems communicate ideas, the way they can feel so truthful and wise.

I began to take notes, to read, to write down thoughts. I kept talking with people, running my ideas by them. I changed my mind, again and again.

In 2007, I met my future wife, Sarah, and then a year later moved to San Francisco, where she lived. I stopped traveling so much, and was able to begin assembling an actual book. As I wrote and rewrote, I discovered that, beyond the elusiveness and the variety of the subject matter, there were fundamentally difficult, even paradoxical obstacles to writing a book about how to read poetry.

For one thing, the act of treating poetry like a difficult activity one needs to master can easily perpetrate those mistaken, and pervasive, ideas about poetry that make it hard to read in the first place. Like classical music, poetry has an unfortunate reputation for requiring special training and education to appreciate, which makes most of us feel (unnecessarily) as if we haven't studied enough to read it. In his widely read introduction to *The Best Poems of the English Language*, Harold Bloom writes, "The art of reading poetry begins with mastering allusiveness in particular poems, from the simple to the very complex." This is not true. The art of reading poetry does not *begin* with thinking about other cultural products, or historical moments, or great philosophies. It begins with reading the words of the poem, which sounds very simple, and is, except that it quickly becomes very interesting. Reading poetry, we need to remember that we are all experts in words; we have been for a long time. And any word we don't know we can look up in the dictionary that will always be beside us when we read.

To learn to read poetry is first a matter of forgetting many incorrect things we have learned in school. And then of learning to accept what is right before us on the page. A big part of what the book needed to do, I realized, was to demonstrate ways of reading poetry that would resimplify and redirect our attention toward the purpose of poetry.

The question was not really *what* poetry is (poems can be so many things), but *why* it is written, and what it does. It seems that our inability to grasp why we are reading poetry, for reasons fundamentally different from why we read all other forms of writing, is what makes poetry so hard to understand.

To explore why we read poetry and what it does, it is necessary to talk about the experience of reading poetry. The problem is, that experience is an elusive one to try to capture in words. For one thing, it differs from person to person, though there are some commonalities about the genre of poetry, its function and effects, that we can discuss. More important, when a person truly falls in love with a poem, it is usually because it feels like a private experience. Moving through the poem, the reader feels a kind of understanding that is hard to paraphrase or resay. Therefore, the essential knowledge of a poem, what can make it feel so necessary, cannot ever fully be put into other words. The better the poem, the harder it is to talk about it.

John Ashbery writes in "Paradoxes and Oxymorons" that experiencing a poem is:

A deeper outside thing, a dreamed role-pattern,
As in the division of grace these long August days
Without proof. Open-ended. And before you know
It gets lost in the steam and chatter of typewriters.

Ashbery's poem points to that feeling of being just on the verge of knowing, and even for a moment *knowing*, something the poem has told us, something vital. But before you can hold on to that knowledge, it is gone, at least until you read the poem again. The experience of getting close to the unsayable and feeling it, and how we are brought to that place beyond words by words themselves, is the subject of this book.

Poetry isn't in any danger, and never has been. It has thrived for the entirety of human history, or at least as long as we have been using language to communicate, and I am quite sure that there will be poetry as long as there are people who can speak, and probably even after. Probably even robots will write it, just as soon as they get souls. No matter what we say about it, or don't, poetry inevitably will (as Auden wrote) keep surviving in the valley of its making.

But for so many of us, that does not seem to be enough. People carry so many incorrect ideas about poetry into their readings of it, ones that ruin the experience before they even get to have it. Also, there is a lot to say about poetry, interesting ways of thinking about it out loud and in writing that can bring us closer to it.

Writing this book, I came to think of my task as bringing us together into the experience of reading poetry, without destroying it. I hoped along the way to clear out some unhelpful ideas about poetry that make that experience difficult to have. I'd like to think that this book is, itself, an example in prose of Keats's famous concept of negative capability: saying no to a certain kind of rigidity in thinking, to open up the creative possibility of a new form of attention, of understanding.

Over years of writing, the book also got more personal and autobiographical, a combination of memoir, analysis, and argument. I discovered that what I was really writing about was the necessity of poetry: why it matters, and how in the personal and public spheres poetry might be able to help us live our lives.

I have always been viscerally resistant to hitch up poetry to the wagon of utility. As John Keats wrote in a letter, "we hate poetry that has a palpable design upon us." Poetry seems to get worse the more it seems interested in lecturing and instructing us, usually about things that we already know and agree with. To think of poetry as useful in a social or political way also struck me as dangerous, in that it threatens to demand of poetry something that prose can do far better, and therefore to argue poetry into extinction.

However, the more I worked on this book, the more I realized that I do, in fact, believe that poetry has social and political uses. This book has become, both implicitly and explicitly, an explanation of and an argument for those uses. The usefulness of poetry has less to do with delivering messages (which we can just as easily get from prose), and far more to do with what poems can do to our language, reenlivening and reactivating it, and thereby drawing us into a different form of attention and awareness.

This book was written not to give all the answers (as if that were even possible), but to be a starting point. Reading it should make it more possible for anyone to find the poems that matter to them. Most of all, I hoped that when I was finished with this book, whenever anyone told me they don't know how to read poetry, I could hand them this book and say, I believe just by virtue of being alive you already do.

THREE BEGINNINGS AND
THE MACHINE OF POETRY

HAD YOU TOLD ME WHEN I WAS YOUNG THAT I WAS GOING TO become a poet, I would have been bewildered. Not only did I not read or care about poetry, but I didn't even really imagine (or wonder) whether there was such a thing as a living poet at all. Poetry was something you did in school. It was old and boring. I never would have dreamed it would become central to my life.

In 1985, I was a senior in a big high school in Maryland. It was spring, English class, time of crushes, time of the dreaded poetry unit. The teacher handed around a list, and we had to pick one poet to write a research paper on. I chose W. H. Auden of the mysterious gender, probably because she or he for alphabetical reasons appeared at the top of the list.

From the library I procured a book and started reading the poems. There was no reason to think I was going to enjoy them. I was not a particularly artistic kid, and I didn't work on our high school literary magazine, or write. Nothing was auspicious. I do not remember opening the book. Yet to this day I still remember reading the first few lines of "Musée des Beaux Arts":

> About suffering they were never wrong,
> The Old Masters: how well they understood
> Its human position: how it takes place
> While someone else is eating or opening a window or just
>   walking dully along

and something just clicked. I can't say I felt I immediately understood everything, but the poem seemed to mean something I could not quite put my finger on, something important to me.

This poem was talking about how real suffering is not dramatic, but takes place in ordinary life, "while someone else is eating or opening a window." It's actually not about suffering exactly, but about how people don't *realize* that suffering is happening all the time, while they are doing their regular activities, "walking dully along." I could definitely relate to this; it seemed right to me. I knew this was true, as many teenagers do.

I did not know who the Old Masters were. Obviously, they were old, and they were masters. So they were in control of things, or thought they were, and had been for a long time, it seemed. As the poem says, they were never wrong, at least not about suffering (so are they wrong now? or are they gone?).

Later I learned Auden was talking about great painters, in particular Bruegel. But when I first read the words "Old Masters," something else came to mind, a more general idea that at one time there were people who knew and were in control, but not any longer. I think it had to do with the feeling of being a teenager, coming into adulthood: that scary and inevitable awakening into the truth about your parents and teachers, that they are not gods or masters at all.

The poem thinks about suffering in a general, distanced, even cold way. The ideas are interesting and sometimes a bit complex, but you don't need anything but your attentive mind and a basic facility with English language to understand what is going on. It's well written, and sounds good when you say it out loud, but there is nothing particularly fancy or "poetic" about the language: it doesn't rhyme, nor is it obviously rhythmic in a way that is any different from good prose.

More than anything else, what I liked about the beginning of this poem, and still do, was something about *how* the poem was saying what it was saying. This effect starts right at the beginning of the poem, with the delay in the subject of the first sentence. The word (and therefore the idea of) "suffering" comes first, and we have to wait a little while to find out who this "they" is who "were never wrong."

So when the Old Masters enter the poem, in the second line, it is grand and exciting, a little theatrical, especially after the line break. We have to wait an extra instant, and our eyes have to travel from the end of the first line to the beginning of the second, to find out the rest of the sentence. Who are they? The sentence seems almost biblical, or at least old-fashioned, the way it is reversed. It makes me feel a certain way about what is being said, that it is serious, and has to do with truths that are not merely contemporary.

I liked other poems by Auden too, such as "A Lullaby," which begins, "The din of work is subdued, / another day has westered /

and mantling darkness arrived," which seemed to me a pretty and sad way of describing the end of the day, the sunset, the darkness coming on. I knew that time of day from the long afternoons and early evenings in my family's own house, after school, before dinner, waiting for my father to come home.

But most of all, "Musée des Beaux Arts." I still love this poem. There's a cruel humor there, which I'm only a little sorry to say must have appealed to the sixteen-year-old me: while people are suffering, "dogs go on with their doggy life and the torturer's horse / Scratches its innocent behind on a tree." The poem describes a painting of the fall of Icarus. The end of the poem still gives me actual chills. The boy with his wax wings flies too close to the sun, despite the warnings of his father, and falls into the water, and no one really cares:

> . . . and the expensive delicate ship that must have seen
> Something amazing, a boy falling out of the sky,
> Had somewhere to get to and sailed calmly on.

It is possible that I identified with that boy, who ignored his father's warnings, and whose suffering seems of no real consequence to anyone. Or maybe I felt like the expensive delicate ship. Or both, or something else altogether, I really don't remember. But for me, an anxious suburban kid afraid of disappointing everyone, the world got suddenly big and strange and full of contradictions that seemed true.

I liked this feeling, and I liked thinking the poem through for myself, without the help of any teachers or books. In fact, even though it was supposed to be a research paper, I wrote it all from my head, for which I was gently chastised. Don't get me wrong, this wasn't some kind of lasting revelation. I completely forgot about poetry for years. But I think, just for a moment, I got the message that I could be in direct contact with poetry, without any kind of intermediary. It was a gift I accidentally received, because I was fortunate enough to encounter the right poem for me, at just the right time, when I was ready. Somewhere deep in myself I understood that there was something only poetry could do, a way only a poem could mean, and that I needed that feeling.

THINKING BACK NOW, I REMEMBER ANOTHER TIME, LONG BEfore I read Auden, one I had completely forgotten, when I had a deep and private experience with poetry. It was 1972, and I was in first grade, in Washington, D.C. I went to Oyster Elementary, a small school just a few blocks away from our little row house. Oyster was bilingual, which meant that we took turns holding up pictures of things (duck, house, ocean) and solemnly saying both the English and the Spanish words.

In the morning when we entered our classroom, it was bright, and in the afternoon the sun was on the other side of the building, leaving our room dark and melancholy. On the windowsill were many books, among them a large one, Longfellow's *The Song of Hiawatha*, with big ornate letters and colorful drawings. I loved to go to the window and read it. Often I would get up when the teacher was talking and just wander over there. This was uncharacteristic. I was an obedient eldest child, a little bit afraid all the time of making a mistake or doing the wrong thing.

Our classroom windows faced east, directly over Rock Creek Park, a mostly wild forested expanse that ran right through the middle of the city. I remember standing next to the window, holding the book, knowing the great park, with its massive stone bridges and trees and river, was very close, right there:

By the shores of Gitche Gumee,
By the shining Big-Sea-Water,
Stood the wigwam of Nokomis,
Daughter of the Moon, Nokomis.
Dark behind it rose the forest,
Rose the black and gloomy pine-trees,
Rose the firs with cones upon them;
Bright before it beat the water,
Beat the clear and sunny water,
Beat the shining Big-Sea-Water.

Now when I read this passage it makes me cringe, because of its offensive primitivism, its fantasy about how Indians thought and spoke. The poem also seems a bit silly in the way it says obvious things (like that the pine trees have cones, and so on). But I must confess I still do love how he calls the lake the Ojibwe knew as Gichigami, and we call Lake Superior, "Big-Sea-Water," an example of how something very familiar can, when it is said in an unexpected way, become new for us again.

It still sounds solemn and good. Saying it out loud, I feel now as I did then the elemental force of the words. Forest, pine-trees, them, water, water, Water. There seems to be meaning in the sounds themselves. Robert Frost writes, "The best place to get the abstract sound of sense is from voices behind a door that cuts off the words." This makes me think of listening to my parents talking in another room, or downstairs. In those hums and murmurs there was so much information about mood, the emotional weather in the house, all to be gotten without hearing a single clear word.

As a child, standing at the window, knowing that right there just on the other side of the walls was the great park, the huge trees, and the river that had cut a deep canyon before the capital city had ever been imagined, the entire system of the poem acted on me, helping me feel an immense, sublime force, something true about the old land that had been here long before us.

For better and worse, with all its tragic, complex, at times misguided and at others deeply intuitive sense of mystery, *The Song of Hiawatha* was my first poem. Many of you must have your own. Let us go then, you and I, where evening spreads itself against the sky. Two roads diverged in a yellow wood. Much have I traveled in the realms of gold. Here is the deepest secret nobody knows. I placed a jar in Tennessee. When I get to be a composer, I'm going to write me some music. My life it stood, a loaded gun. Oh there is blessing in this gentle breeze. I celebrate myself, and sing myself. won't you celebrate with me what i have shaped into a kind of life?

THROUGH MY EARLY TWENTIES, I STILL NEVER WOULD HAVE thought to call myself a poet. In college, I majored in Russian language and literature. Right after graduating, I lived for a year on a fellowship in the Soviet Union, "studying" at Moscow State University, which mostly involved drinking vodka at any time of day, eating possibly radioactive meat, and compiling a highly detailed glossary, now lost, of Russian curse words.

When I came back, I moved to San Francisco, in its beautiful early 1990s inexpensive run-down bohemian doldrums. Tragic love, alcohol, soft drugs, temp jobs, more confusion. My hair was long and various colors. I thought to myself that someday I would write songs. I wrote a few; they were not so good. Without a clear idea of how to move forward, I went to graduate school, at UC Berkeley, for Russian literature.

Berkeley in the 1990s was full of brilliant, attractive young people, and I remember when I first got there just walking around admiring everyone. I had gone to a small college in a rural town in the Northeast, so I found Berkeley's urban campus to be romantic in an exciting, bustling, modern way. I was instantly thrilled to be there, but I also almost immediately realized something undeniable: I did not belong, at least not as a scholar. Basically, I was less prepared, less interested, and less motivated than my brilliant, focused classmates. It was obvious to me the first day I sat for hours in the library, laboriously and poorly translating some highly academic text from Russian to English, that my studies were not destined for success. Many years of unpleasant mediocrity in scholarship loomed.

So there, in Berkeley, in the little room I rented, I started to sit down every day for a few hours to write, without really knowing what I was working on, what I was going to find. It is amazing to me now that I knew to do that. Probably it was just an elemental decision, the only thing left to do besides give up writing before I had even begun. And as foolish and careless as I might have been about everything else in those days, for whatever reason I simply could not *not* try to write.

To my great surprise, what I started writing was poetry. I was already deeply attracted to words, in an unreasoned, almost shameful way. I loved them for their own sakes, for the various things they could do, and for the meanings that could be made when I put them alongside ones they weren't ordinarily next to, or far from ones they are usually near. This pleasure I took in language itself overrode any interest I had in telling stories, or organizing my ideas in a systematic way.

I had always loved language. I was intrigued by the meanings of words, the structure of syntax. Even though along with everyone else I complained, in elementary school I secretly liked diagramming sentences. I liked learning Latin in high school, and memorizing the byzantine verb tenses of French.

What I did not yet understand was that this is where the practice of poetry begins. The desire to write anything begins out of a basic human desire to express oneself, to be heard. Writing poetry in particular also comes out of an inexplicable attraction to the possibilities of the material of language itself, a kind of play.

Yet I was also interested in doing more than just playing around. I wanted to take words and build them into larger structures that would *do something*, something exciting, powerful, even useful. I didn't know how to do this. But I did know the feeling I got when I searched out, and found, poems that I loved. It was like plugging something into a socket, and electrifying my imagination, making me feel I was more aware, empathetic, thoughtful, engaged, alive.

WHEN I WAS FIRST STARTING TO WRITE POETRY, I STILL DIDN'T really understand much about it. I hadn't been an English major in college, nor had I read much American poetry. So I felt simultaneously thrilled, destabilized, and confused. I felt sure there was meaning there, somewhere. I could feel it. But I also often doubted myself, and felt like I was looking in the wrong place, or missing what was really important.

At that time, I had the vague impression that poets used poetic language and techniques to express important thoughts or ideas in a more beautiful or complex or compressed way than prose. That is, there was something about the level of language, its beauty or complexity or heightened qualities, that gave a piece of writing the status of poetry, and distinguished it from prose.

The more poetry I read, and wrote, the more clearly I saw that there really was no such thing as "poetic language." The words in poems are for the most part the same as those we find everywhere else. The energy of poetry comes primarily from the reanimation and reactivation of the language that we recognize and know.

Poetry isn't merely a more beautiful way to communicate ideas or experiences or feelings: prose, after all, does that, and can be just as beautiful as poetry too. I noticed there were, of course, ideas in poetry, but they always seemed just out of reach, somehow both important and also in a way not, or at least not *most* important. Focusing just on those ideas, and trying to say what a poem was "really" about, always felt reductive, as if whatever was most important was being left behind in the act of explanation itself. Poetry seemed to be more about something else, something like creating a different sort of mood, or mental space, or way of thinking.

Ludwig Wittgenstein wrote, "Do not forget that a poem, although it is composed in the language of information, is not used in the language-game of giving information." If not to give information, what is the language of poetry for? What does it do that is different than prose? And why, as readers and writers, do we return to it, and preserve it?

The concept of genre—a defined category of writing, like poetry or novels or plays—isn't currently fashionable. Many people find such categories too restrictive and fussy. Much of the energy of contemporary literature is in crossing and mixing various genres in single pieces of writing. Yet when it comes to poetry, it can help to think about genre in a more isolated way, at least temporarily, because the question of genre is really a question of purpose: Why did the writer choose a certain type of writing, and how does that choice affect how we should read the work before us?

We don't usually need to think about *why* we are reading something. Usually, we have an immediate, intuitive sense of what it is for, and therefore how to read it. Without needing to be told, we understand the difference between reading a novel and reading the newspaper. We know we should be looking for something different in each of those experiences. Stories and novels create characters

and situations and tell stories; journalism communicates informa-
tion; essays engage in that hard-to-categorize effort to explore,
however loosely, a certain idea; editorials and sermons tell us what
we should and should not do, and believe; and so on.

No one can seem to tell us why poems are written, what they
are for. Why are they so confusing? What are we supposed to be
looking for? And what is the point of rhyme, of form, of metaphor,
of imagery? Is it somehow to decorate or make more appealing
some kind of message of the poem? What is the purpose of poetry?

When I am asked such questions, I think of what Paul Valéry
(1871–1945) wrote in "Poetry and Abstract Thought": "A poem is
really a kind of machine for producing the poetic state of mind by
means of words." Valéry's description has always seemed to me to
be as close as anyone has gotten to describing what poems can do:

> *If the term* machine *shocks you, if my mechanical comparison
> seems crude, please notice that while the composition of even
> a very short poem may absorb years, the action of the poem
> on the reader will take only a few minutes. In a few minutes
> the reader will receive his shock from discoveries, connections,
> glimmers of expression that have been accumulated during
> months of research, waiting, patience, and impatience.*

The poem makes poetry happen in the mind of the reader or
listener. It happens first to the poet, and in the course of writing, the
poet eventually makes something, a little machine, one that for the
reader produces discoveries, connections, glimmers of expression.
Whatever it does it can do again and again, as many times as we
need it.

The "poetic state of mind" that poetry makes happen could be
described as something close to dreaming while awake, a higher,

more aware, more open, more sensitive condition of consciousness. The poem makes this happen for us by placing our mind as we read or listen in consonance with the associations being made by the poem: its "discoveries, connections, glimmers of expression."

In a letter, Emily Dickinson wrote, "If I read a book and it makes my whole body so cold no fire can warm me I know *that* is poetry. If I feel physically as if the top of my head were taken off, I know *that* is poetry. These are the only way I know it. Is there any other way?"

I like this answer too because, like Valéry's definition, it distinguishes poetry from other forms of writing not by any particular formal quality—like rhyme, or line breaks, or musicality, or the use of imagery or metaphor—but by its *effect*. Her definition is functional and empirical, passionate and subjective: I know poetry, say Dickinson and Valéry, because of how it makes me feel, what it does to me.

HOW POETRY CREATES THE POETIC STATE OF MIND IN A READER is the central question of this book. It happens through the form of the poem, which guides the mind of a reader. It happens through leaps of association. And it happens as the poem explores and activates and plays with the nature of language itself.

Poems exist to create a space for the possibilities of language as material. That is what distinguishes them from all other forms of writing. Poems allow language its inherent provisionality, uncertainty, and slippages. They also give space for its physicality—the way it sounds, looks, feels in the mouth—to itself make meaning. And poems also remind us of something we almost always take for granted: the miraculous, tenuous ability of language to connect us to each other and the world around us.The elusive, quicksilver, provisional nature of language is by necessity suppressed in ordinary conversation, as well as in most other writing. What makes a poem different from any other use of language is that it remains the sole place designed *expressly* to make available those connections that are hidden when language is being used for another purpose.

Language waits to be released in poetry. Poetry enacts the possibilities and powers that lie dormant in the nature of language itself. Poems are where contradictions and possibilities of the material of this meaning-making system are *deliberately* brought forth and celebrated, ultimately undistracted by any other overriding purpose.

Unlike other forms of writing, poetry takes as its primary task to insist and depend upon and celebrate the troubled relation of the word to what it represents. In following what is beautiful and uncertain in language, we get to a truth that is beyond our ability to articulate when we are attempting to "use" language to convey our ideas or stories.

Poetry takes this inherent limitation of the material of language—that words are imprecise in their relation to whatever it is they all-too-imperfectly denote—and turns it into a place of communion. Remarkably, impossibly, miraculously, we somehow manage to communicate and mean despite the imperfect instrument of language. In this way, the provisional, tenuous, exciting, fragile, imperfect, yet intensely pleasurable relationship of a poem to language, and to meaning, could be said to be a kind of metaphor for our own relation to language, the world, and each other. There can be both sadness and joy in this recognition of the human condition. It could be said the relationship of poems to what we intuit but can never fully say makes them like prayer, that unending effort to bring someone closer to the divine, without pretending the divine could ever be fully known or understood.

When we are attentive to the language of poetry, to the words we see before us in the poem, we start to get a glimmer of the actuality, the paradox and complexity and uncertainty, that lies behind the way we usually perceive the world. Words and ideas can loosen and break free for a moment, so we can experience them anew.

The power of the activated material of language in poetry can only fully be pursued when the writer is not *ultimately* preoccupied with any other task, like storytelling or explaining or convincing or describing or anything else. In their poems, poets do those things, but only as long as it suits them. A poet is always ready to let them go. Every true poem is marked, somewhere, by that freedom. And that choice to be ready to reject all other purposes, in favor of the possibilities of language freed from utility, is when the writer becomes a poet.

2

LITERALISTS OF THE
IMAGINATION

MARIANNE MOORE'S "POETRY," WHICH APPEARED IN HER FIRST book, published in 1921, begins in a way that may cause frustrated readers to nod in agreement:

> I, too, dislike it: there are things that are important beyond all
>   this fiddle.
> Reading it, however, with a perfect contempt for it, one
>   discovers in
> it after all, a place for the genuine.

In its original 1921 version, the poem goes on for several more stanzas. Over the course of Moore's life she kept in various versions shortening it, until the entire poem ultimately consisted only of the lines above, although in her *Complete Poems*, published late in her life, she also printed the original version in the notes at the end of the book, so in the end we have both.

The short version is amusing, but the longer one is far more interesting. In it, Moore writes that the things in poetry are important "not because a / high-sounding interpretation can be put upon them but because they are / useful," and that "we do not admire what we cannot understand." At the end of the poem, she writes that we will not "have" poetry until

> . . . the poets among us can be
>   'literalists of
>   the imagination'—above
>   insolence and triviality and can present
>
> for inspection, "imaginary gardens with real toads in them"

Moore's comparison of a poem to a beautiful, imagined place that contains real things, even ones we sometimes think of as ordinary and ugly, feels accurate to me. To be a literalist (as a poet but also as a reader) with the words in a poem, not to treat them as symbols or codes but to take them for what they are, is what draws us into true strangeness.

Moore's imaginary garden is the world the poem builds, the place where we as readers in our imaginations can go. This garden can be a pretty ordinary place. Or it can be fantastical and otherworldly, like Coleridge's gardens full of incense-bearing trees, in his poem "Kubla Khan." Or maybe there is no recognizable, physical place at all in the poem, which can be more of an abstract space we can go to, in order to think differently, and imagine. Regardless, reading the words literally is how we move into the garden where, as Wallace Stevens writes, we find ourselves "more truly and more strange."

Despite what you might have heard in school, with certain very limited exceptions, poets do not generally deliberately hide meaning, or write one word and really mean another. The stakes are (or should be) too high. Yet so many of us have been taught to read poetry as if its words mean something other than what they actually say.

In this version of poetry, poems are designed to communicate messages, albeit in a confusing way. Everything that is in the poem—metaphors, similes, imagery, sounds, line breaks, and so on—is decorative, that is, placed on top of the message or meaning of the poem. The student's job is to discover that meaning, and to repeat the central (often banal) message or theme back to the teacher, or in the exam. Bonus points are given for showing how poetic elements enhance this message.

Why this should be, and what the point of all this is, is never addressed or explained. It seems this attitude about poetry and poetic language is widespread. I recently read a quote from the makar (an enviable Scottish term for poet laureate) of Glasgow, the evocatively named Liz Lochhead, who said: "The way poetry is taught at the moment is absolutely appalling . . . They teach poetry as a problem, rather than a joy, and that's disgraceful. . . . It's clear that even teachers think poetry is a code. I have been asked by a boy, who e-mailed me once: 'when you wrote that poem about the bull, what did you really want to say?' His education had allowed him to get the misapprehension that a poem is a code trying to get a message across."

In rare cases (such as poems written in times of political oppression, or in particular eras when poetry had agreed-upon symbolic conventions), words in a poem can stand for something specific that is deliberately withheld or hidden. But these are isolated exceptions, and a little historical context and guidance can bring us into these poems as readers.

Regardless of how plainspoken or strange, how realistic or elusive or symbolic or metaphoric the poem is, in order to have any meaningful experience with it at all, the reader must first read very carefully and closely, and think about what the words mean. A good dictionary is almost always all that is necessary.

To be clear, I am not saying that I think all good poetry should be simple. Nor am I saying that poems mean what they say *only* in the most literal sense. I am saying that any meaningful experience with poetry *begins* with first reading literally, more literally than we do any other kind of writing.

If this seems simplistic or too obvious a point to make, trust me, it is not. I have seen time and again, as a teacher and as a poet, that even advanced students, even many poets, do not think to read poetry this way.

So many people assume what is difficult about poetry is that its meaning is hidden, to be uncovered. Yes, reading poetry is difficult, in that it requires some concentration, and slowing down, just as it would to read anything else unfamiliar. But the true difficulty—and reward—of poetry is in reading what is actually on the page carefully, and allowing one's imagination to adjust to the strangeness of what is there. Poetry has different secrets, ones that may be more difficult to accept than to discover.

THE PORTAL TO THE STRANGE IS THE LITERAL. AS A TEACHER, I have found that regardless of how open or resistant my literature students initially are to poetry, all the big progress comes when they start getting literal with the words on the page. I usually ask them, before we even begin talking about what the poem "means," to go to the library to investigate a word in the poem, to find out as much as they can about it. I ask them to use whatever resources they can, including the *Oxford English Dictionary* and anything else, to figure out what the word would have meant at the time for the poet.

They come back with many exciting facts, some of which are not relevant to the meaning of the poem. But the exercise of getting as deeply into the words as possible has the effect of showing them that this is the way into a poem, and that meaning and possibility come from that act, and not from some search for an interpretation someone else already made of the poem, that they have to figure out to get a good grade. My students start to feel a direct, powerful relation to poetry, one that can happen outside the classroom, without an intermediary. They remember that poetry is written in their language, and that all of us can be liberated into our own independent lives as readers.

It turns out that a close attention to definitions and etymologies can be a portal to the power of poetry. This is why, more than a professor or some other priest of literature, a necessary companion for reading poetry is a dictionary.

Mahmoud Darwish wrote: "Extreme clarity is a mystery." Many poets, however, confuse being deliberately obscure with the deeper mystery of poetry. Because we are told that poetry is inherently "difficult," and that by its very nature it somehow makes meaning by hiding meaning, our first efforts at poetry often naturally reflect this.

Good poets do not deliberately complicate something just to make it harder for a reader to understand. Unfortunately, young readers, and young poets too, are taught to think this is exactly what poets do. This has, in turn, created certain habits in the writing of contemporary poetry. Bad information about poetry in, bad poetry out, a kind of a poetic obscurity feedback loop. It often takes poets a long time to unlearn this. Some never do. They continue to write in this way, deliberately obscure and esoteric, because it is a shortcut to being mysterious. The so-called effect of their poems relies on hidden meaning, keeping something away from the reader.

I have also come to see that, in addition to pernicious instruction, there might be certain psychological aspects contributing to the impulse younger poets have to keep their meanings hidden. Some fear feeling exposed. Others are afraid of being seen as banal, or stylistically derivative, or uninteresting, or stupid. These are, of course, more or less the fears of all writers, young and old. I don't know what writers of stories and novels and essays eventually discover for themselves, but I can say that sooner or later poets figure out there are no new ideas, only the same old ones, and also that nobody who loves poetry reads it to be impressed, but to experience and feel and understand in ways only poetry can conjure.

I am sympathetic to young poets who feel a strong impulse to disguise what they are saying. Early in my life as a poet, I had trouble being direct. I was intensely attracted to poets who used clear, simple, elemental language, but also felt somehow that saying something simple and direct, or telling a little story, or being anecdotal or narrative in any way, wasn't "really" writing poetry. I felt self-conscious, and as if I needed to demonstrate my talent and ability with the art in every line. It took me a long time to get over this feeling, and it was only when I did that I started to write poetry that was any good.

I'm sure also I was afraid of inhabiting whoever I was as a poet. I was afraid to be judged. What if I was open about who I was as a poet, and it wasn't any good? What if people thought I was untalented, or mistaken about my vocation? Those fears are naturally very strong in many young artists, and it's really hard not to succumb to them by making art that is clever or formally imitates complex and intellectually challenging work. It's a kind of self-protection.

I see this a lot in the work of my students. Often, unconsciously, they will do something at the beginning of their poems that demonstrates, according to whatever terms they have, that they are poets. It's as if they are presenting their poetic qualifications (licenses?) for inspection at the front door of the poem. Some of them, for instance, will do something really weird and disruptive with syntax. Others will throw in a bunch of images and metaphors, right away, before we even know what the poem is about. There is often recalcitrance about giving basic information about what is going on, where we are, who is speaking, et cetera, as if to do so would be to "ruin" whatever is poetic about the poem. But that sort of superficial introduction of confusion is not how great poetry is made, nor how we are brought closer to what is most difficult to say.

IT IS OFTEN RIGHT AROUND THIS POINT—AFTER I HAVE SAID that poetry is not a secret code, and that it is not written to be deliberately elusive or obscure—that people say: Okay, but what about modern poetry?

T. S. Eliot's long, fragmented, allusive *The Waste Land*, published in 1922, is often brought up as a prime example of the difficulty of modern poetry. Many of us remember being intimidated by this poem, which seems to be a minefield of historical and cultural references, and of confusing, uncontextualized voices in different registers and even languages. It is indeed a difficult poem for most of us to grasp without some kind of context, or guidance.

Eliot and many of his fellow Modernists believed in setting a very high standard for intelligent reading, and thought of themselves as preservers and saviors of a culture in decline. For this reason, they wrote in a deliberately difficult, elusive, and allusive style. Eliot's peer William Carlos Williams presciently saw the potentially dangerous appeal this type of poetry would have, writing that Eliot's poem was "the great catastrophe of our letters . . . the blast of Eliot's genius which gave the poem back to the academics." He could see that certain teachers would gravitate toward High Modernist poems, and use those poems to appoint themselves members of a priestly caste, the keepers of esoteric knowledge.

What can be problematic about a modern poem like *The Waste Land* is not its difficulties per se. It is how the difficulties it presents—such as a reference to an obscure historical event or literary work or something mythological, an unattributed quotation in a foreign language, syntactical weirdness, an esoteric word— can create a great penumbra of imagined difficulty and mystification throughout the whole poem, one that shadows everything, even the simplest and most direct statements. *Everything* about the poem seems difficult to us. We begin to think even straightforward things cannot be what they seem. For many readers who have encountered modern poetry in school, this shadow of difficulty seems to extend, just as Williams warned, to cover all poetry.

Before the beginning of *The Waste Land* there is a short epigraph in both Latin *and* Greek, a quote about an ancient Greek oracle known as the Sybil, from *The Satyricon* by Petronius. Despite what we might have been told by scholars and teachers, our ultimate understanding of the poem does not depend upon this immediate demand for erudition. Yet this demand can be so intimidating and destabilizing that it establishes a certain mentality about reading poetry, such that when the poem itself begins, we might not notice that it is written in plain English that anyone can read:

April is the cruellest month, breeding
Lilacs out of the dead land, mixing
Memory and desire, stirring
Dull roots with spring rain.
Winter kept us warm, covering
Earth in forgetful snow, feeding
A little life with dried tubers.

Think for a moment if this were written in prose. Would you find it confusing? Maybe a bit elusive—what is the point, why is he telling us this?—but not mystifying. There is not a single complicated word in the passage.

The poem begins with an odd, subjective assertion: "April is the cruellest month." Why? Things are starting to come alive again. Our expectations are low in winter: we are just trying to survive. In spring, big things start to happen, "Memory and desire." The "Dull roots" are starting to come to life again, because of the spring rain. The poem talks about the month like it's a person, asserting that it is somehow responsible for "breeding" these flowers—lilacs—out of the dead land. The elements of time— April and winter—are personified, and switch their usual roles, April becoming something cruel and terrible, because it starts to make us aware of some things we might have forgotten: memory and desire.

The brief close reading I just demonstrated of that passage above required no special knowledge, only attention. The meaning of the poem resides on the page, and is available to an attentive reader.

Could there also be a symbolic significance to some of the elements in the passage above? Yes, absolutely, Do we *need* to research April, lilacs, dull roots, spring rain, to "get" the poem? I don't think so. If we do such further investigation, we may discover further resonances, either in Eliot's process (what consciously or less so made him choose these particular objects for the poem, or what he might have been thinking, which is interesting, if ancillary) or in the ways that the elements of the poem interact that might not be obvious at first reading. These speculations and resonances can deepen and even complicate our initial readings. But the central and most important experience of even this difficult poem begins with our own readings, in an encounter with our common language.

IN MY OWN EXPERIENCES LEARNING TO READ POETRY, I HAD TO get used to slowing myself down, and being attentive to every word. This was, and is, challenging for me. I have a tendency to want to race through things, to get to the point or the end, to find out who the murderer was or what the key points are. But you can't read poetry that way. Reading poetry has the salutary effect on me of *forcing* me to read, and think, at a different pace than the rest of my life demands.

Sometimes, when we read poems that seem difficult, we assume they are written in a coded way. Yet even where the words of poetry are used mostly musically and intuitively, the literal meaning of words is always an essential part of the effect. The whole power of the poem, its unparaphrasable mystery, depends entirely on the actual meanings of words.

Surrealist Paul Éluard's barely translatable 1929 poem "La terre est bleue," "The Earth Is Blue," begins:

La terre est bleue comme une orange
Jamais une erreur les mots ne mentent pas
Ils ne vous donnent plus à chanter
Au tour des baisers de s'entendre

Which, in my literal translation, reads:

The earth is blue like an orange
Never an error words don't lie
They don't let you sing anymore
It's the turn of kisses to hear each other

How can something be blue like an orange? Does an orange (the fruit) have a kind of quality of blueness that has nothing to do with its color, something more abstract? Does that quality some-how resemble the way the whole earth is blue? It's a bit maddening and also exhilarating.

The effect of this Surrealist poem depends on the way it takes very seriously the impact of that gorgeous, disorienting first line. "Never an error words don't lie / They don't let you sing any-more." Éluard seems to be saying that it is only when words lie, or when they make errors, that they allow you to sing. Paradoxically, this idea is only available to someone who reads the meaning of the line carefully, who assumes that the words in the poem are not lying, at least not individually. Maybe the necessary lie or error is something more conceptual, having to do with the larger state-ment he has made about the color of the earth, a kind of true lie, a correct error.

Éluard knows that he has glimpsed, if only for a moment, something essential, a truth that is gone. Now he is left only with the response to an unspoken, probably internal objection to the first line: no, it is not an error to say it, words don't lie, I insist, the earth really is blue like an orange. And the third line, to me at least, feels like a reproach, either to the doubting listener (words don't lie, they don't let *you* sing anymore, because you won't let them) or maybe to Éluard himself, who has lost that fleeting moment of insight.

The very first words radioed back on April 12, 1961, by the very first person to orbit the earth, cosmonaut Yuri Gagarin, were "The earth is blue . . . how wonderful. It is amazing." Éluard's prescient line, which seems to anticipate by thirty years the experience of seeing the earth from space, reminds me of the English romantic poet Percy Bysshe Shelley's contention in his essay "A Defence of Poetry" (written in 1821) that poets are seers, and act as "mirrors of the gigantic shadows which futurity casts upon the present."

"La terre est bleue comme une orange," "The earth is blue like an orange," is a line written primarily to produce an effect in us, rather than to communicate information. But producing the effect at all depends on us taking in the elements of the line—"earth," "blue," "like," "orange"—as words, understanding what they mean, and feeling how the meanings of those words in new combinations rearrange our consciousness.

THREE LITERAL READINGS

WALT WHITMAN'S POEMS ARE STRAIGHTFORWARD, EVEN PROSE-like. He writes in a language that Marianne Moore called "plain American which cats and dogs can read." "Song of Myself," the first poem in *Leaves of Grass*, begins, as so many of us remember from school, "I celebrate myself, and sing myself, / And what I assume you shall assume, / For every atom belonging to me as good belongs to you." I don't know if cats and dogs know those words, but most people do.

For the first several sections of the poem, the poet thinks out loud, mostly about himself, and things he has seen, experienced, and thought, all of which make him who he is. He enjoys physical sensations and ideas, sitting out of doors, mentally roaming, proudly loafing. He is drifting, and the poem drifts along. These

casual yet attentive ruminations are suddenly interrupted at the be-
ginning of section six:

> A child said, *What is the grass?* fetching it to me with full
>   hands;
> How could I answer the child? I do not know what it is any
>   more than he.

Anyone who spends any time at all with a child knows the at
times amusing, at others exasperating, pleasures of this sort of mo-
ment. The child comes up to the adult, asking a question that is at
once literal—what exactly is this green stuff called grass, where
does it come from, what does it do—as well as metaphysical: What
is this stuff *for*, why is it here?

There is, I believe, a tendency for us, because of how we have
been taught to think about poetry, to immediately start to try to
read the child as standing in for something (the concept of youth?
mortality? innocence?), and the grass too (the natural world?
growth?), and so on. This type of thinking can easily distract us,
pulling us away from the actuality of the scene being described, in
search of "meaning."

In the poem, grass is grass. Here is an actual child, holding
real grass, asking a particular question to a particular person.
Grass is the familiar green stuff we see everywhere, and the magic
of the poem is how in looking at it this way the grass becomes
not less but more poetic, resonant with meaning. Grass starts to
become for the poet and for us once again as mysterious as it is for
a child.

The poet does not know how to answer the child but, as
adults do when they have the time and energy and good faith,
tries anyway:

A child said, *What is the grass?* fetching it to me with full
    hands;
How could I answer the child? I do not know what it is any
    more than he.

I guess it must be the flag of my disposition, out of hopeful
    green stuff woven.

Or I guess it is the handkerchief of the Lord,
A scented gift and remembrancer designedly dropt,
Bearing the owner's name someway in the corners, that we
    may see and remark, and say *Whose?*

The poet's honest answer to the child's question is that he does
not know, but that he is going to start thinking about it in a specula-
tive way. The grass, when processed through the imagination of the
poet, becomes many different things. First it is "the flag of my dis-
position." The disposition of the poet here is both his personality and
also literally how he is sitting or lying in the grass, which in a sort of
proud anthem of laziness and openness to imagination he describes
right at the beginning of the poem: "I loafe and invite my soul, / I
lean and loafe at my ease. . . . observing a spear of summer grass."

When he compares the grass to "the flag of my disposition,"
the poet for just a moment is in a kind of funny way imagining that
his "disposition" (physical and spiritual) is a country, or maybe
a ship, or some other entity that would have a flag. It's a kind of
exaggeration, a thought that happens when one is not restricted
by appropriateness, or things that are, strictly speaking, true. It is
the first of many strange and delightful and liberated moments of
imagination made possible by following the mind of the poet as he
tries to answer the child.

First, grass is a flag. Then it might be a handkerchief, one belonging to, of all people, God. Grass becomes, in an unexpected connection, a handkerchief the Lord "designedly dropt." The comparison is unexpected, but the more you think about it, the more it makes sense, the more similar the qualities of grass and a scented handkerchief could be said to be. Grass is, as anyone who has ever smelled fresh grass might imagine, "A scented gift."

The grass, like a handkerchief, has been left here on purpose: not by accident, but "designedly dropt" by the Lord. This almost makes it seem as if the field of grass is like a token dropped by a lady, to be found by a knight or gentleman in a romantic novel. There is something strange and sweet about the intimacy of that association, as if for a moment Whitman imagines an almost flirtatious relationship between him and the Lord.

Like many handkerchiefs, this one is monogrammed. It has "the owner's name someway in the corners," though we can't see it. Whenever I read this line, I think anachronistically of DNA, the key and signature to all creation, hidden away in every particle, though of course Whitman did not know anything about this. For Whitman, the grass is something the Lord dropped on purpose so that we would ask the question, to whom does this belong, and thus presumably be for a moment reminded of the divine origin of everything.

The speaker in "Song of Myself" begins to answer the child not by making a scientific, pedantic, botanical explanation about what grass is. Maybe he senses that this is not what the child really wants to know, or maybe he just thinks it would be more fun or interesting or true to try to answer the question in a different way.

It seems right away that he, a little selfishly perhaps, is not thinking so much of an answer that would be interesting for the child. Maybe he is still too busy thinking the way he has been up to that point in the poem, and can't make the transition to child-language quickly enough, or doesn't want to. Or maybe he has very high expectations of the child's understanding. Anyway, the child is not heard from again—perhaps he or she wanders off in search of an adult more willing to goof around, though a part of me (the hopeful poet) thinks that despite the complex answer, the captivating rhythm and mesmerizing charisma of the speaker would have kept the child around for at least a little while.

> Or I guess the grass is itself a child, the produced babe of the vegetation.
>
> Or I guess it is a uniform hieroglyphic,
> And it means, Sprouting alike in broad zones and narrow zones,
> Growing among black folks as among white,
> Kanuck, Tuckahoe, Congressman, Cuff, I give them the same, I receive them the same.
>
> And now it seems to me the beautiful uncut hair of graves.

It has always struck me as being simultaneously mournful and funny that the speaker imagines, in a compensatory way, that the grass itself could be a child, especially when I intuit that the actual child is no longer there.

One of the things I have always loved about this part of the poem is the repetition of "I guess." The poet not only acknowledges but also celebrates the fact that he doesn't actually know. He revels comfortably in speculation. In this way, the poem demonstrates the value of a kind of knowledge that comes not from books but from the imagination. In order to answer the question "What is the grass?" botanically, you'd have to look in a book or study or ask an expert. And that would be useful and interesting. But it would only be a certain kind of knowledge.

WALLACE STEVENS WAS PERHAPS THE UNLIKELIEST OF THE GREAT American poets. By education a lawyer, and by employment an upper-level insurance executive, Stevens continued to work as a vice president at the Hartford Accident and Indemnity Company even as he was gradually becoming the most celebrated poet of his era.

I find the paradox of the life of the businessman/lawyer Stevens intriguing because of his similarities to my own father, also a walking contradiction: a tax lawyer who played guitar and sang, though mostly to himself; a person of deep sensitivity and compassion who could also be ruthless in business; a folk singer in a business suit or a businessman with a guitar—who can really say.

Stevens's poems are abstract, though also often oddly specific, and it can be initially unclear what he is writing about. Sometimes, the poems don't seem to have any subject at all. And he seems to have little interest in everyday life. The events in them seem to take place in a "there," a dreamlike space, not exactly our world, but somewhere else like it.

Stevens's first book, *Harmonium*, was published in 1923. At the time he was already forty-three years old, which would be considered downright ancient for a debuting poet today. Here is a poem from it:

Tea at the Palaz of Hoon

Not less because in purple I descended
The western day through what you called
The loneliest air, not less was I myself.

What was the ointment sprinkled on my beard?
What were the hymns that buzzed beside my ears?
What was the sea whose tide swept through me there?

Out of my mind the golden ointment rained,
And my ears made the blowing hymns they heard.
I was myself the compass of that sea:

I was the world in which I walked, and what I saw
Or heard or felt came not but from myself;
And there I found myself more truly and more strange.

Here we find ourselves in a dreamscape. The title is specific, referring to an event (tea) at a particular place (the Palaz of Hoon), but also slightly off: the spelling "Palaz" feels vaguely foreign, and the location "Hoon" does not exist anywhere in our world's geography. The "I" in the poem is not named, nor is the "you" whom the speaker addresses, who uttered the enigmatic phrase "the loneliest air."

The speaker in "Tea at the Palaz of Hoon" seems to be implicitly comparing himself to the sun, which too descends, or appears to. I always feel when I am reading this poem that I too am descending, down the lines, into a stranger and stranger landscape, transforming. This poem, as one reads it, can feel as if it is actually happening, physically: "What was the ointment sprinkled on my beard? / What were the hymns that buzzed beside my ears?" This is a single, uncanny moment of awareness, like waking up in another body.

The phrase "loneliest air" is, I think, not possible to paraphrase or translate into some other familiar concept, without doing violence to the full possibility of the meanings it creates. In this phrase, air is not just *lonely*, which would be interesting but also in a way merely lovely. This air, as someone has said to the speaker, is the "loneliest" of all air. Perhaps what is being implied is that all air is, by nature, in some way inherently lonely. Empty. I stop for a moment and think about this, that some air can be lonelier, and some the loneliest of all.

Reading this poem can create the very atmosphere it describes: something familiar, but also not, like a very realistic dream. In this place, "there," at the Palaz of Hoon, there is the exciting, disturbing possibility of unfamiliar experiences and feelings. And once the speaker in the poem finds himself "there," he himself becomes not just the passive experiencer of what is happening, but the very source of these great wonders: out of *his* mind the golden ointment rains, *his* ears make the blowing hymns they heard.

And being "there," at the Palaz of Hoon, the speaker finds himself "more truly and more strange." I love the slight dislocation of using the adverb "truly" and the adjective "strange" in a parallel construction. Each time I read the line I feel jarred: Shouldn't he have said more "true," and not "truly," in order to maintain proper grammar?

Yet it is precisely this unusual grammatical construction itself that generates so much of the meaning of the line. To find "myself more truly" refers to a process, the *way* of finding oneself. The feeling of finding oneself "more truly" than before, and the feeling of finding oneself "more strange" (perhaps more strange than one believes one is, especially if, for instance, one is a lawyer and insurance executive), here are completely interrelated. Each causes the other. This mutual causation is an effect of the grammar: saying it more conventionally would take the shimmering multiplicity out of the line.

BECAUSE WE NEED TO NAME THE FEELING WE HAVE AFTER A great loss, we call it "grief." But anyone who has experienced it knows that this is just a word assigned to what is, in its horrible, shifting, massive complexity, unnameable. To push away the accepted name of something, and to move, with careful literality, through the language, in a journey of renaming: this is a courageous act.

Brenda Hillman explains in a short introduction to her 1992 collection *Death Tractates* that she wrote the poems of the book in the time right after her "closest female mentor died suddenly at a young age." The poems reflect that shock of sudden death, and the great emotions that result, while also being weirdly logical, attentive to detail, speculative, and brilliant.

A tractate is a systematic exploration of a subject. The word implies a sustained effort to fully understand something, through a series of attempts. To me the word is most obviously associated with Wittgenstein's early work the *Tractatus Logico-Philosophicus*, for which he wrote the notes while he was a soldier in World War I. In its final form it became a series of very short, often gnomic declarative statements about language, reality, and knowledge.

Like Wittgenstein's *Tractatus*, Hillman's *Death Tractates* is an attempt to logically respond to traumatic events. But Hillman's tractates are far more than logical propositions. They are, together, the sustained record of an individual mind mustering all of its faculties to try to come to terms with a catastrophe. Hillman's book is an effort to rename the feeling we call, approximately, grief.

At the beginning of "Yellow Tractate," she writes:

Smart daffodils! They waited
till the cold snap was over, then brought themselves
into the corridor, like lamps of pity—

I have never heard anyone say "lamps of pity" before, nor have I ever heard anyone compare daffodils to lamps of anything, though when you look at a daffodil, you can see that they do, in fact, look a lot like that. The poet sees things in the world transform into other things, and this seeing happens in language, in metaphor. Flowers become lamps of pity, and, in the way of all metaphors, all the elements refract with new meaning in relation to each other. Flowers are lamps, lamps have pity, flowers have pity, pity has flowers.

The more I read this passage, the more I love that odd word "corridor." We usually think of a corridor as having to do with buildings or trains, a passageway in an interior space. But a secondary meaning, the one used here, is of a long narrow piece of land. The word "corridor" actually comes from the Latin word for "to run," and probably has to do with something military, the way a group of people would have to move quickly, in peril, through a narrow strip of land to get from one place to another. If we look deeper into the word "corridor," we will know the poet is walking outside. But for most of us our first association will be with an interior space, a hallway. I believe the poet was drawn to this word precisely because of this duality, its claustrophobic connotation.

Whether or not the poet knew all this about the word "corridor," I very much doubt she was consciously aware of it while writing this poem. When a poet writes, she feels instinctively if a word is correct. She could easily have written other words there: the daffodils could have brought themselves into the meadow, into the field, into the garden, and so on. But the poet's brain chose "corridor," she knew it was the right word, probably because it is in a sense the wrong word, the word we were not anticipating. This is what Aristotle meant when he wrote, in *The Poetics*, that poets are those who have "an eye for resemblances"; that is, for seeing similarities and connections that others do not.

The poet often makes the choice of a word based on the way it sounds, as if it "fits," for reasons the poet at the moment might very well not be able to articulate. The way a word sounds "right" to a poet has to do with something much more than only sound itself: it is the resonance of all the meanings the word has carried and accumulated over thousands of years. The ear of the poet is not merely attuned to sonic music. It is attuned to the music of ideas in words, the latent resonances, the ones always waiting in etymology, the pasts of words, our individual pasts, and our collective memory.

Because of this, and because of all the reading and thinking poets have done about words and language, and their intense love of the material of language itself, poets just "know" when something is right, in the same way Cézanne from his intimate lifetime relations with paint "knew" that splotch of green had to migrate above his right eye in *Self-Portrait with Palette*, or the composer knows the oboes at a certain moment absolutely must start doing whatever oboes do.

Hillman's poems are difficult in that they ask us to be closely attentive to the meanings of words, to read slowly, to think about the resonances of what is being said and, most important, to accept the hidden connections between things. The poet is deeply endeavoring to be scrupulously honest to the actuality of the loss. For her, this is an authentically strange and difficult experience. She is trying to talk very honestly into the face of something that resists language. Here is how the book begins:

First Tractate

That the soul got to choose. Nothing else
got to but the soul
got to choose.
That it was very clever, stepping
from Lightworld to lightworld
as an egret fishes through its smeared reflections—

through its deaths—
for it believed in the one life,
that it would last forever.

The more attentive we are to what this poem is actually saying, the more dangerously close we can get to feeling the poet's grief. The "it" in these first two stanzas, that stepped like an egret and believed it would last forever, is the soul of the departed.

The soul, like the egret, "fishes through its smeared reflections." Today, on my walk around Lake Merritt, where I live, I saw a snowy egret (a small white bird with a black beak) doing exactly that. It has yellow feet, and very seriously and slowly hunts looking down at the water, sneaking up on something we can't see. Of course the word "egret" is so close to "regret."

The bird is not just fishing through its reflections, but "through its deaths." Here the poet is probably wondering for a moment whether every kind of change (from moment to moment, as the reflection in the water changes, and then changes again) is a kind of death. If so, maybe the death of the body, and the movement of the soul from one state to another, is just another kind of change. The "First Tractate" continues:

When she had just started being dead I called to her.
Plum trees were waiting to be entered,
the swirling way they have,
each a shower of
What.
Each one full of hope,
and of the repetitions—

When she had been dead a while
I called again. I thought she was superior somehow
because she had become invisible,
because she had become subtle
among the shapes—

and at first she didn't answer; everything answered.

The poem has become much more casual, anecdotal, less strictly logical. It is almost as if with this first line of the third stanza, "When she had just started being dead I called to her," the poem begins again. This makes a lot of sense. It feels very close to the circular and repetitive nature of grieving. The whole book will be a series of attempts to write into this loss, over and over again.

The plum trees (common to the Bay Area, with their bright purple canopies) seem to be a place where the poet for a moment imagines she could go, a place to get lost, maybe to forget. But her terrible confusion does not allow her even a moment of solace. Entering the plum trees would leave her with the same great questions: Where is my friend, where has she gone, why was she taken from me.

Even ordinary phenomena like trees and leaves and fruit seem unnameable to her. The book will be a struggle to keep coming back to language, to naming, and as readers we go through that process too, of continually coming back into language, ourselves experiencing many moments of struggling, then finding the name. This linguistic struggle in the poems is a representation of the general mechanisms of grief. Grief can silence us, but to grieve through, we have to speak.

That moment in the plum trees, with the capital "What," reminds me of Dickinson, because of the capital letter, and the use of the dash, and probably also because of the word "called," one of the two words written on Dickinson's tombstone: "Called Back." Often I used to visit her grave in Amherst, Massachusetts, when I was first studying poetry, to ask for help or just put a little trinket on top of her gravestone (what she called in one of her poems "her granite lip"). Perhaps in my worst, most desperate moments, I expected her to answer. In the poem, the departed does not answer, but everything else does.

4

MAKE IT STRANGE

IN 1917, THE RUSSIAN LITERARY SCHOLAR, ESSAYIST, NOVELIST, and memoirist Viktor Shklovsky wrote "Art as Technique," in which he boldly attempts to explain, precisely, what makes something not merely an informative text, but a work of art. Shklovsky was one of the great independent thinkers of the early Soviet period. At various times he was a soldier, a revolutionary, and an exile. After his stormy early years, he returned to the Soviet Union in 1923 and lived the rest of his life, until 1984, in relative obscurity.

According to Shklovsky, artistic texts use the exact same language as texts designed primarily to convey information, but do something different with it. The specific mechanism by which language becomes not merely a conduit to convey meaning, but something more, is called, in Russian, "*ostraneniye*," most often translated as "defamiliarization," though a more literal translation would be something like "strangeifying."

Shklovsky describes how, as we go through our daily lives, our perceptions of things become "habitual" and "automatic." We start to lose the sense of the actuality of things, and treat them as abstractions.

> *Habitualization devours work, clothes, furniture, one's wife, and the fear of war . . . And art exists that one may recover the sensation of life; it exists to make one feel things, to make the stone stony.*

This habitualization in life is mirrored in (or perhaps even caused by) our use of language: we start forgetting the true significance of words and using them quickly, thoughtlessly, to function socially, and to stand in for certain experiences. Habitualization is (to borrow a Marxist term) a kind of "false consciousness." Poems can return us to an understanding about language, and the world, that is related to the most basic truths of existence.

Through art, language and therefore experience become "defamiliarized," so we can feel and experience anew:

> *The purpose of art is to impart the sensation of things as they are perceived and not as they are known. The technique of art is to make objects "unfamiliar," to make forms difficult, to increase the difficulty and length of perception because the process of perception is an aesthetic end in itself and must be prolonged.*

Poetry exhibits the purest form of defamiliarization. This is because in a poem, other tasks, such as telling a story, or fully and exhaustively expressing an idea, never take priority. Therefore, it is in poetry that we see most clearly and powerfully, without any other ultimate distraction, how language can be made deliberately strange, how it becomes especially "a difficult, roughened, impeded language," in order to jar us awake.

OTHER WRITERS HAVE ALSO NOTICED THIS SAME PHENOMENON, the tendency of experience (and language) to become habitualized, and the possibility literature gives us to see things again in new ways. Gertrude Stein asserted that because she wrote "a rose is a rose is a rose is a rose," once again "the rose is red for the first time in English poetry for a hundred years " George Orwell's 1946 essay "Politics and the English Language" presciently links habitualized uses of language to a debased political culture. And when Emerson wrote in his 1844 essay "The Poet" that language is "fossil poetry" because long ago, "each word was at first a stroke of genius . . . because for the moment it symbolized the world to the first speaker and to the hearer," he was also noticing that one thing poetry can do is to remind us of a time when we were, as a species, in a sort of childlike state of perpetual wonder.

In the first of his famous *Letters to a Young Poet*, Rilke comes upon his own definition of defamiliarization, when he counsels his correspondent to "pretend you are the first man and then write what you see and experience, what you love and lose." Rilke knew it is good for poets to know a lot about language, and then to genuinely and deeply take on the task of becoming innocent in relation to it again, to feel its great, complex power. This is good advice for readers too.

In one of Dickinson's oft-quoted poems, "Hope" is defined as "the thing with feathers / That perches in the soul." A "thing with feathers" is, of course, a bird. But saying it that way, as if it is unfamiliar, and needs to be described again, causes us to rethink those qualities of a bird that resemble hope, and in turn to rethink hope. Just imagine how, if the poem just said " 'Hope' is a bird / That perches in the soul," we would be immediately in the land of Hallmark cards. Describing a bird as if she didn't know the name for it, and assigning its qualities to the abstract concept of "hope," is the defamiliarizing technique of the poem. It has an almost clinical unsentimentality, an objectivity of insight that feels trustworthy, won from hard thinking.

One short, simple poem whose effect comes from defamiliarization is by Langston Hughes:

Suicide's Note

The calm,
Cool face of the river
Asked me for a kiss.

The imaginative act of describing water as having a face is old. Many of us have heard it many times from the second line of the Old Testament, "And the spirit of God moved upon the face of the waters" (King James). This metaphor of the face of the waters exists in the original Hebrew version of the text. In Hughes's poem, he takes what is a very familiar imaginative act—the water has a face—and treats it literally, as something that could, like a real face, ask for a kiss. And this request, which the suicide feels compelled to grant, becomes the explanation for the self-annihilating act.

MY SENIOR YEAR IN COLLEGE, I LIVED IN AN OLD DORMITORY on a hill, a few hundred yards away from the house where Emily Dickinson had lived most of her life. What I thought I knew about Dickinson was actually vague and anecdotal: that she was a weird recluse who had never left her home, or read anything except the

Bible and the Anglican hymnal *The Book of Common Prayer.* As far as I knew, she had written her poems on little scraps of paper and died in obscurity.

Much later, after reading her poems and letters, I learned that she was a far more complex character than she is usually portrayed to be. She traveled, read plenty, and knew a tremendous amount about history, geography, science, and flora and fauna. She corresponded widely, and sent her poems to friends and family and strangers. Later in her life she stayed mostly at home, but she was far from being a lifelong hermit. In her own idiosyncratic way, she was very much a poet of the world.

In her nearly 1,800 poems, she considers great concepts directly, and also follows small observations, or experiences, like seeing a plant or animal, or taking a walk with her dog, Carlo, into moments of vast realization. Death was one of her most common subjects. Here is one of her best-known poems, written in the summer of 1862:

> I felt a Funeral, in my Brain,
> And Mourners to and fro
> Kept treading—treading—till it seemed
> That Sense was breaking through—
>
> And when they all were seated,
> A Service, like a Drum—
> Kept beating—beating—till I thought
> My mind was going numb—
>
> And then I heard them lift a Box
> And creak across my Soul
> With those same Boots of Lead, again,
> Then Space—began to toll,

As all the Heavens were a Bell,
And Being, but an Ear,
And I, and Silence, some strange Race,
Wrecked, solitary, here—

And then a Plank in Reason, broke,
And I dropped down, and down—
And hit a World, at every plunge,
And Finished knowing—then—

The poem begins with a simply written sentence. The poet is making an initial imaginative leap: it feels to her in this moment that there is, actually, a funeral going on in her brain. She writes that she *felt* this funeral, which is an odd phrase. I've been to, and heard about, a lot of funerals, but never really *felt* one, especially not inside my head. Or maybe, now that I think about it, I actually have. I remember at my father's funeral, as soon as I saw the plain pine box, putting my head down and not looking up until it was over. I sensed what was around me, and heard the words of the eulogies, but only as a kind of distant, muffled noise.

In this way I *felt* it. I must not be the only one. This might be why so many readers have found that phrase so memorable. But the connection so many readers feel to this poem is, I think, in something more than just the recognizability of the description, an effect which after all could also be achieved in prose. There is something about the elemental simplicity of the familiar words in the poem, how they become ominous and *felt*, by being placed in a poem that does not merely describe but *enacts* the situation. Words we think we know—the ones associated with death—come horribly alive again.

Dickinson was, like the people of her time, surrounded by frequent death, the physicality of it. When she was young she lived for a time next to a graveyard, the one in which she would eventually be buried. She saw funeral processions all the time. People didn't live nearly as long then, and often succumbed to what would now be minor diseases or syndromes. The physical facts of mortality, including the objects and procedures of funerals themselves, were quite real to her, more than to most of us.

It's not hard to imagine how death could, through its constant presence, have become mundane. One of the main purposes of Dickinson's poem could be said to bring herself, and us, close again to the reality of death. In the third stanza, she feels the "Box" (with the unmentioned and unmentionable body in it) being lifted and carried across her soul, which, by implication, becomes a physical space, a kind of room, with a creaking floor. In feeling the funeral, as if for the first time, physically inside her, she starts to become painfully aware. Sense and Silence have a concrete reality in this world. She is, along with Silence, shipwrecked. What may be most mysterious about the poem is the unsayability at the end of the poem, which ends in the middle of a thought, with the small, ominous "then."

THE CLOSER WE GET TO THE MOST DIFFICULT EXPERIENCES IN life, the more a great simplicity in language seems to be required, and the more difficult it is to attain. The temptation is overwhelming to attempt, and inevitably fail, to comfort others and ourselves with platitudes. It's hard to know what else to say.

This may be why many of the greatest poems about death are unadorned. They help us to confront what is happening, with the most precise language we can summon, to see it in its strangeness again. If we do not have the strength or will to summon that precision of language for ourselves, whenever we are ready, poetry can help us.

This poem by the Spanish poet Antonio Machado (1875–1939) seems to me elementally simple, mortal, strange, and true:

At a Friend's Burial

They gave him earth one horrible afternoon
in the month of July, under the fiery sun.

One step from the open grave
there were roses with rotting petals
among sour smelling
red geraniums. The sky
pure and blue. A strong
dry breeze was blowing.

The two grave diggers
lowered the coffin,
hanging heavily from thick ropes
to the bottom of the grave . . .

And on resting it made a loud thud,
solemn in the silence.

The blow of a coffin on the earth
is something perfectly serious.

Heavy dirt clods broke
on the black box . . .

The air carried
white breath from the deep grave.

—And you, shadowless now, sleep and rest,
long peace to your bones . . .

Finally,
sleep a still and true sleep.

There are only so many ways to place a body into the earth. And it always makes the same sound. Too many of my students know this sound and, once they realize this poem is actually about that moment, will often become solemn and recede into their own memories of loss. The poem is no longer merely an intellectual or academic exercise.

The poem begins with a clear, unsentimental description of the funeral. There is one oddity of the phrasing, right at the beginning of the poem: "They gave him earth." This is a good translation, because it is close to the original: in Spanish, the line is "*Tierra le dieron una tarde horrible.*" It is just odd enough, without sounding pointlessly weird. The translators (Carmen Scholis and William Witherup) chose wisely in not normalizing this phrasing, making it something like "they gave him to the earth" or even "they put him in the ground." They kept the peculiarity of the phrasing in the original, though unfortunately in English the ambiguity of the Spanish pronoun "*le,*" which could mean either "he" or "it," is lost, which means we don't get the implication that this "he" is still he, but has at the same time also become an "it," a lifeless body.

There is no escaping the actuality of death and burial in this poem: the roses with rotting petals, the heavy coffin, the thud, the silence, the clods of earth, and that amazing moment when the dust from the grave for a moment seems to the poet to be "white breath," when of course it cannot be. We want to believe the dead are sleeping. But even in the deepest sleep there is of course the movement of breathing, and at the end of this poem we have sleep that is "still," total, and true. Reading this poem, I think there is the suggestion that what keeps us alive is a kind of provisionality and imperfection. Alive, our sleep is not totally still, not totally true, and it is only in death that we find the resolution and sureness and finality that we might so often crave in life, without realizing its connection to death.

THE PARTICULAR AWAKENING TO LANGUAGE THAT POETRY CAN bring is more than merely a private matter. It is an ethical one. Earlier, I mentioned Orwell's 1946 essay "Politics and the English Language," in which he writes that language "becomes ugly and inaccurate because our thoughts are foolish, but the slovenliness of our language makes it easier for us to have foolish thoughts." He connects idiomatic language to "concealing or preventing thought." Poetry, when it is focused on this need to reawaken us to the actuality of language, can take on a political dimension.

A famous and harrowing poem from Adrienne Rich's classic 1973 book *Diving into the Wreck*, "Rape," reawakens us to that terrible and all-too-familiar word. For a long time we have heard the word "rape" used figuratively, to describe everything from what we are doing to the environment to experiences of nonsexual violation, regardless of how serious.

Roxane Gay, in her 2011 essay "The Careless Language of Sexual Violence," points out how we have become desensitized to that word. Her essay justly critiques an infamous article (published a few weeks before Gay's essay appeared) in the *New York Times* that described the gang rape of an eleven-year-old girl in Cleveland, Texas, by eighteen men. It's a horror that any sane person would naturally want to turn away from, and Gay writes that the author of the story did exactly that, focusing on "how the men's lives would be changed forever, how the town was being ripped apart, how those poor boys might never be able to return to school," and not on the victim herself.

Gay points to the author's avoidance of the use of the word "rape." Instead of it, he used the term "sexual assault," or wrote that the victim was "forced to have sex." Gay writes, "Language, in this instance, and far more than often makes sense, is used to buffer our sensibilities from the brutality of rape, from the extraordinary nature of such a crime." Gay goes on to advocate for a recapturing of the actuality of this crime in our writing, advocating "ways of rewriting that restore the actual violence to these crimes." The poems that do so have already been written and, tragically, will continue to be.

Rich's poem brings the terrible actuality of that word back. The poem is addressed to an unnamed you, clearly a woman who is reporting a sexual assault to an unsympathetic, patriarchal policeman: "you have to turn to him, / the maniac's sperm still greasing your thighs, / . . . you are guilty of the crime / of having been forced." Here is how the poem begins:

> There is a cop who is both prowler and father:
> he comes from your block, grew up with your brothers,
> had certain ideals.
> You hardly know him in his boots and silver badge,
> on horseback, one hand touching his gun.
>
> You hardly know him but you have to get to know him:
> he has access to machinery that could kill you.

The "machinery that could kill you" is of course the aforementioned gun, but later, when that line is repeated, it also becomes language itself, the power to write down a report that will be either believed or ignored.

> You hardly know him but now he thinks he knows you:
> he has taken down your worst moment
> on a machine and filed it in a file.
> He knows, or thinks he knows, how much you imagined;
> He knows, or thinks he knows, what you secretly wanted.

He has access to machinery that could get you put away;
and if, in the sickening light of the precinct,
and if, in the sickening light of the precinct,
your details sound like a portrait of your confessor,
will you swallow, will you deny them, will you lie your way
 home?

The repetition of the lines in the final stanza awakens us to
the actuality of the scene, taking us out of mere description. And
there is something about repetition itself in this poem that does feel
sickening: this has happened before, and will happen again. The
simple, stark title of the word alone makes the poem an essential
redefinition of the word, like an entry in a dictionary. The word is
not having the effect it must. And the only beginning to a solution
is for us all to become reawakened to its actual, horrible meaning.

WHEN THEODOR ADORNO FAMOUSLY ASSERTED THAT WRITING
poetry after Auschwitz was barbaric, it was because he understood
that a pervasive, deliberate obfuscation of words was inextricably
connected with the Nazi program. A systematic misuse of words
allowed the German populace to tell themselves lies and comfort-
ing stories. For Adorno, to do anything to obfuscate the truth in
speech or writing is far more than improper: it is to implicitly par-
ticipate in the same process that made the Holocaust possible.

In *Eichmann in Jerusalem*, Hannah Arendt described in detail
how a fundamental deceptiveness in language was essentially re-
lated to making the murderous behavior of the Nazis, as well as the
German population's acceptance of their acts, possible. The Ger-
man problem with language has also been explored in fascinating
and horrifying detail in several books by the late journalist Gitta
Sereny. Sereny's *Into That Darkness: From Mercy Killing to Mass*

Murder, is based on more than sixty hours of interviews she conducted with Franz Stangl, the commandant of the death camp Treblinka. The book is a singular reading experience. Stangl, one of the few men to have been in charge of a Nazi extermination camp, rationalizes his own behavior through clichés and lies and official language and explanations, until at the very end of the interview, he admits his guilt, and dies of a heart attack nineteen hours later. He was, it seems, literally keeping himself alive through his own deceptions.

To live morally, to avoid self-delusion and even monstrosity, we have to think about what we are saying, and to avoid euphemism and cliché. Pope Francis, speaking in July 2013 on the small island of Lampedusa, Italy, where so many North Africans have drowned trying to make their way north across the Mediterranean, said:

> *Today no one in our world feels responsible; we have lost a*
> *sense of responsibility for our brothers and sisters. We have*
> *fallen into the hypocrisy of the priest and the Levite whom*
> *Jesus described in the parable of the Good Samaritan: we see*
> *our brother half dead on the side of the road, and perhaps we*
> *say to ourselves: "poor soul . . . !" and then go on our way.*
> *It's not our responsibility, and with that we feel reassured,*
> *assuaged. The culture of comfort, which makes us think*
> *only of ourselves, makes us insensitive to the cries of other*
> *people, makes us live in soap bubbles which, however lovely,*
> *are insubstantial; they offer a fleeting and empty illusion*
> *which results in indifference to others; indeed, it even leads*
> *to the globalization of indifference. In this globalized world,*
> *we have fallen into globalized indifference. We have become*
> *used to the suffering of others: it doesn't affect me; it doesn't*
> *concern me; it's none of my business!*

For Pope Francis, this is as much a language problem as a spiritual one. Even when confronted with the direct evidence of someone else's suffering, we are able to say to ourselves "poor soul," and simply by saying it to "feel reassured, assuaged." Our own language thereby falsely comforts us. And it is our insensitivity to the language of others, "the cries of other people," that leads to "the globalization of indifference."

Like Pope Francis, and Orwell, and Arendt, Adorno is absolutely correct about the relationship between imprecision in language and harmful self-delusion. But Adorno's admonition about poetry rests on a fundamentally incorrect assumption. Poems are not where the meaning and directness of language are hidden from us. To write them is not barbaric, but the contrary. Poems are the place where the actuality of language and of life is most made available. And it is up to us not to evade it.

5

SOME THOUGHTS ON FORM
AND WHY I RHYME

WHEN I FIRST STARTED WRITING POETRY, I WAS NATURALLY thinking not just about what I was writing, but about how, and why. Why did poems look the way they did on the page? Why did poets make those decisions to break lines or not, write in rhyme and meter or in free verse, and so on? What was the *correct* way to write poetry?

When I decided I wanted to try to write poetry "seriously," whatever that would mean, I gravitated toward poems that were in form. I went to Cody's bookstore on Telegraph Avenue, and bought the *Norton Anthology of Poetry*, a giant black tome that looked like it had all the answers.

I still have that same volume: it starts with "Anonymous Lyrics of the Thirteenth and Fourteenth Centuries," and Chaucer, and ends 1,400 pages later with poets born in the 1940s. At the end of the book there is an appendix, "Versification," which has a list of poetic forms and their principles. These were of great use to me as a beginning student of writing poetry. Not unlike the forlorn geometric shape in Shel Silverstein's *The Missing Piece*, I set out systematically to write each one, in search of where I belonged.

For about a year, working my way through that appendix, I embraced the possibility that writing in rhyme and form would solve the problem of how to make a poem: follow the instructions, and learn how to write formal poems better and better, until I would become "a poet." I carried around a rhyming dictionary, writing terrible sonnets, lousy sestinas, atrocious villanelles, abys-

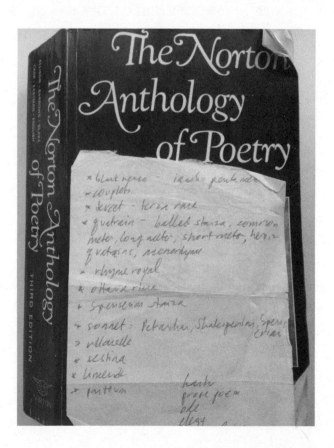

mal pantoums. I felt like I was working, and was, which was good, but it was also painful and embarrassing. I didn't realize then that I was doing my own clumsy version of what art students do when they learn to paint. Now, whenever I go to the museum I usually see at least one of them with a sketchbook, copying the great paintings, and it makes sense to me.

What I was searching for, without knowing it, was a reason for the form of poems. It was only through a long apprenticeship, and through much experimentation (and failure), that I began to discover why poems look the way they do on the page.

The creation of the poetic state of mind in poet and reader is inextricably connected with form. A poem, literally, makes a space to move through. To read a poem is to move through that constructed space of ideas and thinking.

When this is working, the mind of the reader goes in a more or less easy unison along with the poem. This can be an odd, exhilarating, disturbing experience, almost like being haunted or possessed, when the associative, drifting way the thoughts and ideas move in the poem takes over our mind, and makes us feel both troubled and reassured, changed and also more ourselves. As we think along, we start to make connections, and have experiences and feelings we might not have otherwise had without the poem. To read a poem can be a kind of seemingly impossible communion, with someone far away in time and space.

This movement of the mind through a poem—the mind of the poet in creating it, and then the mind of the reader in experiencing it—always takes place as a process in time. Our mind moves down the page, in close unison with the mind of whatever consciousness is speaking in the poem, which takes however many seconds or minutes. In an interview in the *Paris Review*, poet Anne Carson describes this way a poem unfolds:

CARSON: Some people think that means the poet takes a snapshot of an event and on the page you have a perfect record. But I don't think that's right; I think a poem, when it works, is an action of the mind captured on a page, and the reader, when he engages it, has to enter into that action. His mind repeats that action and travels again through the action, but it is a movement of yourself through a thought, through an activity of thinking, so by the time you get to the end you're different than you were at the beginning and you feel that difference.

INTERVIEWER: So it's an action for both the writer and the reader.

CARSON: Yes, exactly, and they share it artificially. The writer did it a long time ago, but you still feel when you're in it that you're moving with somebody else's mind through an action.

A poem presents itself as a kind of real-time movement of thinking, down the page, which the reader can enter, and follow. This can feel like something between watching a movie and listening to someone think out loud.

As Carson implies, this isn't merely a contemporary style: poetry has always been a record of the movement of the mind. This is true of the great poetry of human history, from the fragments of Sappho to the ancient Chinese poets to the thirteenth-century Persian mystic Jalal Rumi. It is true of Shakespeare's sonnets, that allow us to follow complex argumentation and reasoning as it moves down the page. It is true of the poems of the great English Romantic poets, who, as Wordsworth wrote, believed that the poem is the record of a great emotion, later "recollected in tranquility," and reproduced so that a reader can experience it. And it is true as well of the even more distilled, even fragmented, records of the movement of the mind in Symbolist and Surrealist and much contemporary poetry.

When Virginia Woolf wrote, "The poet is always our contemporary," she meant that poets have always made spaces that, however specific to time and place, in some way feel common to human experience. Poems are not, in the end, always contemporary only because they describe the things that happen to all of us: that is a description of literature in general, what makes fables and stories written long ago readable today. Poems are common to human experience because they trace the movement of thought, which, despite the radical alterations in daily human life over the past thousands of years, still remains essentially unchanged.

Often in textbooks and in teaching, the formal elements of a poem, like rhyme, meter, sound, are treated basically as enhancements to the so-called message of the poem. That type of analysis is based on a mistaken idea about what poets do with language and form. It implies that the formal qualities that make a poem what it is are secondary to the main purpose, the central message. If that were true, it would be reasonable for a person to think of those enhancements as unnecessary, even irritating, and to ask why a poet doesn't just say something more simply and directly.

THIS SEEMINGLY SIMPLE POEM BY WILLIAM CARLOS WILLIAMS has baffled so many over the years:

> so much depends
> upon
>
> a red wheel
> barrow

glazed with rain
water

beside the white
chickens.

What does it *mean*? What is it *about*? For decades teachers have asked what it is that "depends" upon this rural scene. Lots of different answers are hazarded by students: The poem is "about" the importance of agricultural life in America, for instance. Or maybe all the elements of the poem, the "wheel barrow," the "rain water," the "white chickens," stand in symbolically for something else, and the poem is "really about" something else entirely.

Regardless of what else can be said about this poem and what it might mean, it is certainly noticeable that the poet deliberately separates phrases that would, in prose, always go together—"wheel barrow," "rain water"—as well as the adjective "white" from the noun it refers to, "chickens." If this same language appeared in prose—"So much depends upon a red wheelbarrow glazed with rainwater beside the white chickens"—it would seem unremarkable, even banal. With a kind of visual defamiliarization, the line breaks slow us down, so we can see what we would otherwise surely pass by. In this way the machine of the poem is, through its mechanisms (the line breaks), *doing* what it is *saying*: asserting the importance of something, a moment, that we would otherwise never see.

Okay, but still: What is this poem *about*? What is important about this little scene, that so much depends on it? What depends on what? Occam's razor applies. The "answer" to what the poem is saying is actually right there. What depends upon these things? So much. The poem is saying that this scene, which seems ordinary, is actually important. "So much depends / upon" it.

The poem itself is an encounter with an ordinary moment in life that suddenly feels significant. This experience, I think, has happened to each of us, at the most unexpected times. This is one of those moments, a feeling of great import that is interesting precisely because it doesn't really have an explanation.

Like so much poetry, this poem insists far more on the *fact* that this scene is important, rather than specifying exactly in what ways it is important. Robert Frost, who was a farmer and therefore intimately familiar with rural life, probably wouldn't have even noticed this scene. But Williams, a town dweller and city lover his whole life, is distant enough from a scene like this one to be struck by the unlikely, yet to him irrepressible, fact of its importance, something others who are more used to it might miss.

Poetry is the way we perceive this importance. The line breaks and filmic way this ordinary scene is parceled out to our consciousness by the mechanism of the poem slow us down long enough for us to see once again what has become too familiar. That is the "message" of the poem. Frankly, as information, the fact that "So much depends / upon" this scene may not be particularly interesting. It may even be banal. But what the poem is doing, what it is for, is not really communicated by the sense of the words. It is enacted by the form of the poem. We *know* "so much" depends on this rural scene, because the poem tells us so. But we truly *understand* that this is the case not because we are told, but because we *feel* it as a result of the form of the poem.

AS WE CAN PERCEIVE FROM THE TERMINOLOGY, TO BREAK A line is to do something unexpected, even violent or unnatural. Different types of line breaks do different things to the mind of the reader. They cause the reader's consciousness to follow along with (and in some ways even, for a moment, become) the thinking mind of the poet. This can sometimes be an aggressive intrusion, and at other times a more casual, less perceptible one. A line break can make us immediately, even frighteningly, aware of the limits of our ability to describe the world.

> I felt a Funeral, in my Brain,
> And Mourners to and fro
> Kept treading—treading—till it seemed
> That Sense was breaking through—

There is regular, if odd, rhythm and off-rhyme in this first stanza of Dickinson's poem. There is structure and order, yet also a great tension, a suspense at the end of each line. What potentially dreadful realization is coming next? That break after the last word of the third line, "seemed," has the dramatic quality of a horror movie: What is going to happen when the tension and pressure of these "Mourners" treading—treading—through her brain become unbearable?

It is easy to see the difference between the poem by Dickinson, with its relatively aggressive use of the line break, and the technique of Walt Whitman, whose easy, strolling, conversational tone is enacted in the long lines and nearly prose-like line breaks of "Song of Myself":

> A child said, What is the grass? fetching it to me with full
>   hands;
> How could I answer the child? I do not know what it is any
>   more than he.
> I guess it must be the flag of my disposition, out of green stuff
>   woven.

Or I guess it is the handkerchief of the Lord,
A scented gift and remembrancer designedly dropt,
Bearing the owner's name someway in the corners, that we
    may see and remark, and say Whose?

This verse has a regularity, with lines that end in an orderly fashion, usually at the end of sentences, or at the very least at the end of phrases, and the stanzas organized into little idea clusters, so that it is easy for us to think along with Whitman for a moment, and then move with him to the next separate, but related, thought.

THE PRESENCE OF LINE BREAKS DOES NOT AUTOMATICALLY make something a poem: just put a piece of prose into lines, and while you might occasionally get lucky and discover something that looks and feels like a poem, for the most part the breaks will just seem arbitrary. This is true regardless of how great the prose writer is. Aristotle wrote in *The Poetics*: "you might put the works of Herodotus into verse, and it would still be a species of history."

Likewise, as much as we connect line breaks with poetry, the absence of them does not disqualify something from being poetry. As early as the 1860s (at the same time Whitman and Dickinson were writing), French poet Charles Baudelaire was writing pieces that were posthumously published as *Little Poems in Prose*, or *Paris Spleen*. These pieces are clearly poetry.

Baudelaire needed to free himself from the strictures of high art and literature, the sense of nobility and grandeur and seriousness which French formal poetry at the time inevitably communicated to readers. He took the drastic step therefore of rejecting all poetic convention entirely, including rhyme, meter, and even line breaks, creating the oxymoronic "prose poem" as a place where even without those poetic devices he could still make poetry happen:

> A room that is like a reverie, a room truly soulful, where the stagnant atmosphere is lightly tinted with rose-colour and blue. There the soul bathes in idleness, made fragrant by regret and desire. It is a thing of twilight, bluish and roseate; a dream of delicious pleasures during an eclipse. The furniture is formed of elongated, prostrated, languishing shapes. The furniture appears to be dreaming; it seems endowed with a somnambulistic life, like vegetables or minerals. The cloth materials speak a silent language, like flowers, like skies, like setting suns.
>
> *("The Double Room")*

"The Double Room" certainly has some of the familiar qualities of prose: it is written in sentences, and describes a situation. The poem even reminds me, just a bit, of the work of Baudelaire's future compatriot Proust, in the way it so successfully creates atmosphere. But the experiences of reading Proust and Baudelaire are obviously different. Even in Proust's *In Search of Lost Time*, a drifting, associative novel, we find characters whose fates we care about, settings to which we return, and other consistent, familiar mechanisms of story.

Unlike prose, the prose poem is freed of any responsibility to consistency. Whatever consistency of setting this prose poem does have is subordinate to a greater purpose, one that has nothing to do with the mechanisms of story. The purpose of the poem is above all else to create an atmosphere: it is to enact the feeling of starting, impossibly, to understand what it is that makes up the human soul, which is, contradictorily, both "bluish and roseate."

The soul is a "thing," and it is "of twilight." Made of twilight? Belonging to it? The poem is beautifully, gracefully, reaching for a feeling about the soul that is, inherently, just out of reach, and in the moment of reading the poem we feel close to, without ever truly reaching, an essential understanding.

When we see prose, we are used to reading for information, to be told a story, and so forth. In a prose poem, the contrast between the mundane form of prose and the unexpected feeling of coming upon poetry can create an all the more startling and powerful reading experience. The presence of this feeling of poetry, without all of its usual signifiers, reveals something about what is central to the poetry, beyond anything specific about its form. Even without the external qualities we recognize as typically poetic, Baudelaire is making the machine of poetry.

And there is a kind of exciting imaginative aggression in the temporary foray of a poet into prose, a Trojan horse, a momentary assertion that poets are capable of reanimating language not just where it is expected, but everywhere.

IN GRADUATE SCHOOL, I WAS READING THE GREAT RUSSIAN AND Soviet poets. Every one of them, from Pushkin to Akhmatova to Tsvetaeva to Mayakovsky to Mandelshtam to Pasternak to Brodsky, wrote rhyming poetry. I loved those poems, and this engagement with rhyme seemed difficult and worthy.

The limited amount of English-language poetry I had read in high school and college had been for the most part formal: it either rhymed or was in some kind of regular meter or both. Even the few twentieth-century poets I had read wrote in forms of some kind or another. One of the poems I had liked best when I read it in college, Eliot's "The Love Song of J. Alfred Prufrock," rhymed, albeit in a not totally predictable way.

As I learned from my Norton anthology, for most of Western literary history, poems had been written either in some kind of rhyming pattern, or in a repeating rhythmic structure, or sometimes both. Shakespeare's sonnets, for instance, rhyme, and also have a regular meter. Other poetic works don't rhyme, but have a consistent rhythm called "blank verse," like Milton's great epic poem *Paradise Lost* and Shakespeare's plays. So the history of English-language poetry seemed at first to confirm my notion that there was an inherent connection between poetry and rhyme, or some other predictable, repeating structure.

On the other hand, I knew there was something called "free" verse. I had heard that term, and had read some poems that didn't rhyme or seem to have any regular or repeating meter. I had heard free verse poems read by poets like Robert Hass and Gary Snyder, at readings upstairs in Cody's Bookstore on Telegraph Avenue, at the Poetry Flash Reading Series, which was my main source of information as a young poet about contemporary poetry. When I heard or read a free verse poem, it felt like poetry to me, and I liked that feeling. But I was also suspicious of it. It seemed too easy, not as hard as writing something that rhymed.

Going to readings at Cody's was very romantic. You'd come off the busy street with its college kids and jewelry hawkers and pamphleteers and panhandlers, and walk through the store and climb the stairs, feeling like a member of some secret club, or an early Christian following the drawing of the fish. There were never any huge crowds there, not even when someone really famous was reading. It felt very intimate. R.I.P., Cody's Bookstore.

Once or twice I went with a friend, but mostly I showed up by myself. I didn't really know anyone there, but people were always nice to me, and a few even recognized me after a while, and would say hello. After the reading I would go get a coffee, usually at the legendary Caffe Mediterraneum. A sign above the main register claims that this is where the caffe latte was "invented." I always called it "The Med," because that's how I heard the locals refer to it. Only much later did I learn that this is where, as legend has it, Allen Ginsberg wrote parts of "Howl."

What Snyder and Hass and so many others read aloud on those evenings in Berkeley did not rhyme, nor was it in a regular, traditional rhythm. But even though they sounded talky and familiar, their poems felt somehow more ceremonial, formed, noble than regular, everyday language. There was a subtle yet irrefutable difference between what they were doing and the regular, everyday language I heard and spoke outside, on the street or in my classrooms or among my friends, the speech that surrounded me.

The story is often told as if, in the good old days, everyone wrote poetry that rhymed (which is why everyone read it), but now that poets have given up and started writing free verse, it's not real poetry anymore. This is an anachronistic fantasy. Milton, in his 1674 preface to *Paradise Lost*, gets quite annoyed by the idea that the presence of rhyme somehow makes a poem. He writes that it is "no necessary Adjunct or true Ornament of Poem or good Verse." He goes on to call rhyme "the Invention of a barbarous Age, to set off wretched matter and lame Meter," and notes caustically that the use of it causes "some famous modern Poets, carried away by Custom, but much to their own vexation, hindrance, and constraint to express many things otherwise, and for the most part worse then else they would have exprest them."

In 1855, Walt Whitman published *Leaves of Grass*, and it changed American poetry forever. *Leaves of Grass* contained poems that neither rhymed nor had a regular, repeating metrical pattern.

These were not the very first free verse poems, but were almost, and they became one template for a certain kind of American free verse (Dickinson's poems, which do rhyme but have a more fragmented and compressed syntax, became another). *Leaves of Grass* marked a great change in American and world literature. It took several decades for poets to assimilate its lessons, but by the early part of the twentieth century, poets had begun regularly to break free of forms, of rhyme and rhythm, by imitating Whitman or other experimental poets or by devising their own ways of writing.

Early in the twentieth century, poetry written in forms was already beginning to seem old-fashioned to many people, even while some of our greatest and most widely read poets (Frost, Bishop, Hughes, Lowell, Moore, and others) were still writing in forms of various kinds. Early twentieth-century Modernism was a great blow to traditional forms in all the arts, including poetry. T. S. Eliot's great early poem and landmark of Modernist writing "The Love Song of J. Alfred Prufrock" (1920) rhymes throughout, but in terms of form, it can be considered a transitional work, looking back toward more formal verse while also pointing in its looser form and tonalities toward the future. Sometimes the rhymes are masterful, as when the fog of the city becomes in the imagination of the poet a kind of feline beast, that "Slipped by the terrace, made a sudden leap / And seeing that it was a soft October night / Curled once about the house and went to sleep." At other times goofy, overly predictable rhymes seem to be making a joke of rhyme itself:

> And indeed there will be time
> To wonder, "Do I dare?" and, "Do I dare?"
> Time to turn back and descend the stair,
> With a bald spot in the middle of my hair—

[They will say: "How his hair is growing thin!"]
My morning coat, my collar mounting firmly to the chin,
My necktie rich and modest, but asserted by a simple pin—
[They will say: "But how his arms and legs are thin!"]

The poem alternately ironizes and embraces rhyme, as if to show a mastery and respect for it, while also bidding it farewell.

By the middle of the twentieth century, formal poetry had definitely ceased to be the dominant mode. Of course, even as free verse became more common, there were, and continue to be, major American poets who use rhyme and/or meter. But the contingent of American poets writing in free verse is today so dominant that it's notable to see a poem that rhymes or is in a strict, regular meter published in a major magazine.

Referring to Eliot's poems, Wallace Stevens in 1948 wrote:

It is like the voice of an actor reciting or declaiming or of some other figure concealed, so that we cannot identify him, who speaks with a measured voice which is often disturbed by his feeling for what he says. There is no accompaniment. If occasionally the poet touches the triangle or one of the cymbals, he does it only because he feels like doing it. Instead of a musician we have an orator whose speech sometimes resembles music. We have an eloquence and it is that eloquence that we call music every day, without having much cause to think about it.

Contemporary free verse poets continue to explore that space between overt formality and casual speech, often getting quite close to one or the other. There is always something different, and thrilling, about the speech in a poem, something that marks it as both connected to and separate from everyday uses of language. In the end, the poems we do not merely admire for their technical facility or beauty, but actually love, are the ones where we recognize the language and also feel a difference.

WHEN DICKINSON (WHO COMPOSED EVERY SINGLE ONE OF HER poems in both rhyme and meter) wrote, "After great pain a formal feeling comes," she was expressing a deep truth about human nature, and writing. Form is the literary expression of our need to be consoled by some kind of order. This is why funerals have rituals and procedures, so we can keep it at least a little bit together in times of great grief and disruption. We don't have to reinvent every single procedure: we can fit ourselves into something ancient, reliable, and true.

I have heard formal poetry read at many a funeral, and it feels exactly, sadly, solemnly right. Occasions of great joy also welcome structure, as any wedding planner will tell you. Even partisans of free verse are likely to turn to poems that rhyme or are in meter to consecrate their marriages.

The uncanny thing about rhyme is that when it is done with casual grace, even and especially when it is simple, it seems as if the words "belong" together, that they were ordained to be connected. In his unfinished and unpublished monograph "Rhyme," the late critic Hugh Kenner discusses a famous couplet by Shakespeare, from *Cymbeline*, "Golden lads and girls all must, / As chimney-sweepers, come to dust." He writes that the rhyme is not surprising, and that is precisely what gives it its power. Though the words are not related etymologically, through being placed together in the poem by rhyme, they *feel* so related that it is "like confronting the wisdom of our vanished ancestors . . . Men once upon a time, we are half persuaded, took great care of naming, and kindred names go with kinship of perception." This is the feeling that rhyme can give us: that things are connected in ways we do not ordinarily perceive.

Poetry reanimates the poetic origins of words. It does so, as Emerson, Shklovsky, Stein, Rilke and many others have pointed out, by making us see language, and therefore things, again as if they are new, and also by reminding us of those "kindred names," those connections we have forgotten. The connections are unexpected, but when they are made, they feel true. Rhymes are just one version of this type of connection: metaphor, associative connections, juxtaposition, and other basic mechanisms of poetry make these sorts of connections too. That is why poets use them, to find the truth buried in our language.

Nowadays there's no way to rhyme in poetry and not sound a bit out of time. Our world is too conscious of the different space rhyme and meter create. This doesn't mean great formal poetry can't be written today. In fact, the difference between it and the rest of our speech makes it surely necessary. I love coming across a beautifully written formal poem, and encountering a speaker who is slightly more formal than, and therefore productively separate from, the overwhelming contemporaneity of our lives. There's enough room in the world of poetry for formal and free verse poems alike.

When I look back at the formal poems I was earnestly trying to write in Berkeley in my early twenties, I can see now they are bad not because they are "old-fashioned," but because that tone of formality was not authentic to my poetic spirit. It did not allow my poems to move or leap or associate in the particular ways they needed to. My formal poems are essentially poor imitations of the superficial aspects of the styles of others. If there are any moments that are true and good in them, they exist not because of, but despite, the formal elements. Poems in rhyme and meter don't suit my mind or the way it needs to move. It's like style: it might seem cool every once in a while to wear a vintage suit, but the fact of the matter is it just doesn't work for me.

One thing I do notice about my poems, written in free verse, is that, though they might not have overt formal elements, there is always a rhythm that develops, subtly, in the voice of the speaker. Maybe something more like a cadence, something closer to what Stevens called "speech [that] sometimes resembles music." Most poetry is somehow "formal" in that way.

And I secretly think my poems actually do rhyme. It's just that the rhyme is "conceptual"; that is, made not of sounds but of ideas that accomplish what the sounds do in formal poetry: to connect elements that one wouldn't have expected, and to make the reader or listener, even if just for a moment, feel the complexity and disorder of life, as well as what Stevens called the "obscurity of an order, a whole." Rhyme is sonic association. Like a metaphor, or a leap in a poem, it connects things we did not expect to be connected yet seem, in retrospect, plausibly or even inevitably linked.

Free verse and rhyming poetry are often said to be in opposition. But, really, they are just different versions of what poetry does. Just as a rhyming poem is built up out of a pattern of repeating end sounds, in some pattern or even irregularly, a poem can rhyme conceptually: that is, through ideas that relate in some way, obvious or hidden. Through their redness, "rose" and "fire truck" rhyme conceptually, as do "deconstruction" and "deep sea diving" (Jacques Derrida and Jacques Cousteau). It can not only be fun to conceptually rhyme, but also be good practice to write formal poems that use conceptual, as opposed to sonic, rhymes. A poem that seems too static because it is locked into a single idea, or a rigid expository framework, can often become both looser and also more true when the poet allows ideas to rhyme conceptually. Conceptual rhyme is not merely a pleasure for poets, but very close to the purpose of poetry, to provide a place for associative thinking.

The excitement of intuitively and attentively moving from one idea or object or memory to another in a poem, and then another and another, and in doing so discovering connections one did not consciously realize were there before, is a great pleasure of reading and writing poetry. Poems are the place where we can feel free to make those connections.

This is also why a poet doesn't ever need to worry too much about plots, or characters, or consistency, or completeness: a poet keeps those structures as long as they help move the poem along, and then at any moment throws them away in favor of the pleasure and excitement of making unexpected and also right-feeling associations. This is what John Keats meant when he wrote in a letter, "with a great poet the sense of Beauty overcomes every other consideration, or rather obliterates all consideration." Each poet has her or his own sense of beauty and connection and association in language, and the only job a poet ever has is to follow that sense, and make the true rhymes, sonic or otherwise, of poetry.

6

THE ONE THING THAT
CAN SAVE AMERICA

ON THE COVER OF THIS POCKET-SIZED EDITION OF JOHN ASH-
bery's *Self-Portrait in a Convex Mirror*, the poet stands in a doorway.
He wears the somehow simultaneously ill-advised and completely
stylish ensemble of a half-unbuttoned patterned shirt and tight
beltless pants. Looking closer, the doorway seems to open not to a
room or to the outside but to a closet: on a shelf behind him there
is a pot or urn, and the flatness of the photograph makes it seem a
bit as if he is wearing it on his head, like a bizarre hat. He is look-
ing straight out of the front of the book, with a direct, slightly fur-
rowed expression. He is about to smile beneath his full mustache.
Something strange is just about to happen.

When I bought this copy of *Self-Portrait*, in 1993, I had just
begun a doctoral program at UC Berkeley. Full of a desire, secret

to everyone including myself, to live a creative life, I was skeptical about, but also attracted to, poetry. Now, holding this same book in my hand, I remember that time, and how Ashbery's poems at first didn't seem to make any sense, or go anywhere, or do anything. I felt angry reading them, as if I were in the presence of a giant literary hoax that I had the choice either to sanction or to condemn. The situation felt profoundly *ethical* to me. The poems offended my sense of what poetry, and art, should do.

I remember how I carried into the reading of the book all the notions I had gathered, from my education and upbringing, about art. And also how I felt, despite my anger and resistance, like the poems somehow were addressed to me. That the poet not

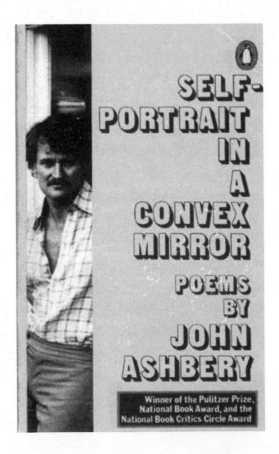

only needed to say these things but also needed someone to hear them. Something huge and important was at last beginning. What I thought was my principled resistance to meaninglessness was really a fear of, and attraction to, a new life.

Here is the first stanza of the poem that changed my mind about Ashbery, and therefore about contemporary American poetry, and I guess therefore my life:

The One Thing That Can Save America

Is anything central?
Orchards flung out on the land,
Urban forests, rustic plantations, knee-high hills?
Are place names central?
Elm Grove, Adcock Corner, Story Book Farm?
As they concur with a rush at eye level
Beating themselves into eyes which have had enough
Thank you, no more thank you.
And they come on like scenery mingled with darkness
The damp plains, overgrown suburbs,
Places of known civic pride, of civil obscurity.

"Is anything central?" Because of the title, this is presumably a question about America, about the one thing that can save it, though how or even from what we do not know. Someone seems to be worried about something, something important yet elusive. The poem seems to be guided in a distracted way by the notion of centrality, searching for it in odd places, unsystematically. Is the one thing that can save America, whatever is "central," maybe located somehow in these otherwise unremarkable places, Elm Grove, Adcock Corner, Story Book Farm? Or maybe in the names themselves?

The names rush into the mind of the speaker as he sees them. They "concur with a rush at eye level," as if he is moving in a car or a train. "Concur" stands out to me: it's odd here, and I'm sure I've never heard it used in a visual sense. The way he sees the towns and their names suggests to him an idea, reflected in that word "concur." "Concur" has a tone of formality, and seems to carry with it the idea of independence along with agreement. The names don't completely merge together, nor remain completely separate.

Everything is all mixed together, and he cannot discern what is central, what is important, which makes him tired. It is not only his eyes, but eyes in general, all of our eyes, "which have had enough / Thank you, no more thank you." I feel a collective exhaustion, a desire for all of our eyes to close.

The poem refuses to directly answer its own initial question. The poem is drifting, and so is the speaker. But the poem does also feel as if something is holding it together, not an answer, but the question itself, the one that begins the poem, and then is asked again more specifically—"Are place names central?" That search for centrality echoes through the whole poem.

The elements of the poem collect together, remaining distinct, accumulating into a feeling that is palpable, but impossible to summarize. It feels, in this first stanza, something like a mixture of nostalgia, melancholy, dread, and peacefulness. These feelings are contradictory, yet they coexist in his mind and mood, and therefore in us as we read the poem.

WHEN I FIRST ENCOUNTERED ASHBERY'S POEMS, THEY PUSHED me into an unfamiliar, exciting, troubling space. I wanted to be there, in that place, so much, and also resisted it. The more I allowed myself to attentively drift, to let go of a certain way of reading, in order to allow a new way to emerge, the more excited and uncomfortable I felt.

Reading his poems required me to give up on looking for a certain kind of meaning that I was used to locating. In my reading, I had always been quick to find the main point, the central idea, which made me one of those annoying students who was always first to raise his hand. Ashbery, and poetry in general, was asking something different of me, a different kind of attention.

I think this is one reason why Ashbery is often thought of as difficult or elusive. It can seem to readers either like there is nothing there, or that they are missing something. "The poem is sad, because it wants to be yours, and cannot," he writes in another poem, "Paradoxes and Oxymorons," which begins:

This poem is concerned with language on a very plain level.
Look at it talking to you. You look out a window
Or pretend to fidget. You have it but you don't have it.
You miss it, it misses you. You miss each other.

That sums up how many people feel reading poetry. A few years ago, I participated in a program called Letters in the Mail, run by the writer Stephen Elliott through his website The Rumpus. To subscribe, you pay five dollars each month, and then every few weeks receive a copy of a letter written by a different author. I had written a letter about being a poet, along with a new poem. I included my mailing address, and some subscribers sent letters back in response. Here is what one person wrote in a letter back to me:

Poetry has always been a drifting experience, like it's floating in the wind and I'm watching it, trying to grasp it back, to hold it, and look at it, and comprehend it. It is always out of reach. I keep thinking I'll understand or love it with the next poem I read. That I only need one more and then I'll "get" it. Alas this seems untrue for me.

I love this letter, because it directly and movingly encapsulates the mixture of longing and confusion that many people feel in relation to poetry. As she says, she feels there is something she needs to "get," though by putting this in quotation marks she seems to know that this very attitude about poetry is, in some way she cannot quite discern, problematic, maybe even the entire problem.

This drifting feeling she describes so well is what a reader can experience, and might have an instinct to resist. When we release ourselves from the need to boil the poem down to a single meaning or theme, the mind can move in a dreamlike, associative way. This associative movement in poetry can at first feel disorienting, but it is actually quite close to the way parts of our minds, unbeknownst to our conscious selves, constantly function, simultaneously attentive to the outside world, but also thinking, processing, half dreaming.

In his book *Conversations on the Frontier of Dreaming*, psychologist Thomas H. Ogden calls this constant and natural state of the mind "reverie," where "playing and creativity of every sort are born; where wit and charm germinate before they find their way (as if out of nowhere) into a conversation, a poem, a gesture, or a facial expression." We become consciously aware of this reverie, a dreaming-while-awake, only rarely: maybe in certain particular situations, such as in a psychoanalytic session, or when we realize we are daydreaming. But, as Ogden writes:

> *The internal conversation known as dreaming is no more an*
> *event limited to the hours of sleep than the existence of stars is*
> *limited to the hours of darkness. Stars become visible at night*
> *when their luminosity is no longer concealed by the glare*
> *of the sun. Similarly, the conversation with ourselves that*
> *in sleep we experience as dreaming continues unabated and*
> *undiluted in our waking life.*

Reverie is just beneath the surface of our moment-to-moment existence. It is our brain's way of processing experience, before it moves to a place of availability. It's where we have been when we suddenly realize we have somehow been driving in complete safety for a few minutes, without remembering any of it. Or when we lose focus in the middle of a conversation, a meeting, a class. It is something that is always going on, while our conscious minds are active and engaged.

We usually are not aware of this process, but it is crucial to how we make sense of the world, and how we understand our place in it. It is, as Ogden writes, "at the very core of what it means to be alive as a human being."

Poetry is a constructed conversation on the frontier of dreaming. It is a mechanism by which the essential state of reverie can be made available to our conscious minds. By means of the poem we can enter this state of reverie with all our faculties alert and intact. Poems make possible a conscious entry into the preconscious mind, a lucid dreaming.

Poems are there, waiting, whenever we feel we need our minds to think in a different way. We can go into the poem whenever we like, as many times as we want, with full alertness. We can be aware of reverie while it is happening, and can hold on to that experience in the poem. Reading the poem allows us to achieve, consciously, a particular kind of very precious awareness.

So often in school or textbooks the vital importance of this state of reverie created by poetry is never addressed. This can leave a reader feeling as if the dreamlike state a poem can create is somehow a flaw, rather than an effect to be treasured for its own sake. In this way, the very desired effect of poetry becomes something a reader can criticize herself for.

The subscriber's letter to me continued:

*I wondered about telling you how poems keep their mystery
as I read them. I wondered if I should tell you I own poetry
books, but cannot seem to read them. I thought more about if
I should tell you that I'm not sure what the poem you sent to
me means. If I should tell you I sat on my bed one night and
read the poem aloud to myself, swatting at the lines buzzing
around my head, eventually laying it down to go to sleep,
putting your poem to sleep as well.*

*It makes me wonder if I'm "doing it" wrong, poetry, that
is. It makes me long for a literature class again where poems
were discussed and analyzed. Maybe that would make me
love them.*

I want to write her back with some useful words. Mostly what
I would want to tell her is that if the poem gave her that "drifting
experience," it is doing what it is supposed to do. I would like to
say to her this experience she describes is precious, rare, virtually
extinct even, and that she has everything she needs already, and is
starting to do it exactly right on her own. And that the preservation
of this drifting experience is the purpose and promise of poetry.

AS SOON AS I WRITE THOSE WORDS, "THE PURPOSE AND PROMISE
of poetry," I feel more than a bit absurd. We live, I believe you will
agree, in desperate times. The seas are rising and so are the gates of
the rich. Maybe it's all America's fault. There seems to be no way
forward, and the problems are almost laughably huge in propor-
tion to our ability to implement even minor solutions. What can
poetry do to save America, us, anything?

In early May 1941, Wallace Stevens, American poet and insur-
ance executive, explored the question of the relevance and neces-
sity of poetry in a lecture, "The Noble Rider and the Sound of

Words." At the time the news from World War II was for the most part very bad. We had not yet joined the war, but our allies were being defeated by an ominous force. It's not hard to imagine the sense of daily, pervasive dread that came to Americans along with the news.

Stevens's talk is an argument for the imagination, and for the necessity of poetry as a particular mode of thinking, especially in difficult times. He writes about how it feels when the news is over-whelming, calling it "the pressure of reality." "By the pressure of reality," Stevens writes, "I mean the pressure of an external event or events on the consciousness to the exclusion of any power of contemplation."

What follows is a passage that seems as if it could have been written today, about our lives:

> For more than ten years now, there has been an extraordinary pressure of news . . . at first, of the collapse of our system, or, call it, of life . . . and finally news of a war. . . . And for more than ten years, the consciousness of the world has concentrated on events which have made the ordinary movement of life seem to be the movement of people in the intervals of a storm. . . . Little of what we have believed has been true. Only the prophecies are true. The present is an opportunity to repent. This is familiar enough. The war is only a part of a war-like whole.

I think, were he alive today, Stevens would have written about the pressure of the real coming from a different sort of news: environmental destruction, worldwide class conflict and inequality, the pervasive threat of national or even global financial collapse, skirmishes always about to escalate into greater conflicts, terrorism, drought, planes falling out of the sky, guns everywhere . . . all those vast forces, somehow both caused by us and also controlled by no one, that have the power to sweep over all of our lives.

Stevens believes the preservation of the imagination, contemplation, what I would call drifting, is not a luxury. It is vital to our survival. This is not a retreat from reality or the world around us. He does not say that a possible poet must be capable of resisting or evading *reality* or the real, but the *pressure* of the real. In fact, the real, freely reimagined and recombined, is precisely what comprises the stuff of poetry. As he writes, "the all-commanding subject-matter of poetry is life."

Here is how Stevens describes the role of the poet:

> *What is his function? Certainly it is not to lead people out of the confusion in which they find themselves. Nor is it, I think, to comfort them while they follow their readers to and fro. I think that his function is to make his imagination theirs and that he fulfills himself only as he sees his imagination become the light in the minds of others. His role, in short, is to help people to live their lives.*

Stevens writes that the poet makes his or her imagination that of the reader, and "sees his imagination become the light in the minds of others," by taking language, with which we are all so intimately familiar, and using it to build a space of contemplation and imagination. The poem is a space any attentive reader can enter, to experience "the poetic state of mind," characterized by something like a state of waking dream, a great attention charged with the possibility of new and elusive connections.

For Stevens, the poem is a reconfiguring of the elements of the real into new forms, ones that help us understand our lives and ourselves in different, necessary ways. In poems, as in dreams, the ordinary is rearranged, reconfigured. In a dream this happens unconsciously. The poet transforms the material of the real in a more-or-less conscious way, in order to create a space of contemplation and imagination and possibility. Again, this is not an escape from the world around us, but a different sort of engagement.

Ashbery's poems, for instance, are full of familiar phenomena and language, often situations or language we recognize from other parts of our lives and do not ordinarily think of as "poetic." One of his early poems, "The Instruction Manual," begins:

> As I sit looking out of a window of the building
> I wish I did not have to write the instruction manual on the
>   uses of a new metal.
> I look down into the street and see people, each walking with
>   an inner peace,
> And envy them—they are so far away from me!
> Not one of them has to worry about getting out this manual
>   on schedule.

From that mundane beginning the poem moves into a long vision, a kind of astral, out of body, meandering journey to and all around a foreign city, one that both describes and creates the poetic experience in a reader:

> And, as my way is, I begin to dream, resting my elbows on
> the desk and leaning out of the window a little,
>   Of dim Guadalajara! City of rose-colored flowers!
>   City I wanted most to see, and most did not see, in Mexico!
>   But I fancy I see, under the press of having to write the
>   instruction manual . . .

Resisting creates a vacuum, into which the poet can freely move. Many marvelous things then occur, as the poet speculates on the life and inhabitants of this city he has never visited, and is therefore free to drift through, imagining.

Being in the contemplative, imaginative, free space a poem provides is, for Stevens, enough. In and of itself the creation of this place is what helps us live our lives. While I think this is true, I also think that this free, imaginative thinking, when applied to the great problems that face us, can help us in other ways as well. Here, for instance, is a poem from W. S. Merwin's 2016 volume *Garden Time*:

After the Dragonflies

Dragonflies were as common as sunlight
hovering in their own days
backward forward and sideways
as though they were memory
now there are grown-ups hurrying
who never saw one
and do not know what they
are not seeing
the veins in a dragonfly's wings
were made of light
the veins in the leaves knew them
and the flowing rivers
the dragonflies came out of the color of water
knowing their own way
when we appeared in their eyes
we were strangers
they took their light with them when they went
there will be no one to remember us

Without mentioning it directly, this poem is obviously concerned with threats to the environment, and the consequences of human behavior on the natural world. Dragonflies are becoming more rare, and are maybe on their way to being extinct. When they are gone, people won't even know what they are missing. The assertions of the poem about the physical nature of the dragonflies— that their veins are made of the same light, that the veins of the leaves know them, that the dragonflies came out of the color of the water—are not, strictly speaking, true. In the poem, though, they become true in a deeper sense.

The dragonflies become physical representations of a natural world in peril, and also a way that the natural world communicates with itself. Their absence becomes emblematic of the great threat we face. The simultaneously dreamlike and attentive space this poem draws us into can help us not merely to understand, but to *feel*, what is happening in the world. The poem ends on a pessimistic note, but it is also possible to imagine reading this poem and, in becoming more afraid, feeling a desire to begin to do something.

WHENEVER I READ "THE ONE THING THAT CAN SAVE AMERICA," I feel Ashbery is helping me to live my life, by making my imagination his, and his mine. I think this is because the poem is glancingly engaged with the sorts of big ideas and issues an American (especially one like me, who grew up in Washington, D.C., and has always been curious about government and politics) might well be interested in, like civic engagement and the nature of American identity, without ever directly addressing them. It's as if the poem is a kind of echo of an unstated big thought, one that is both essential and impossible to exactly articulate, or maybe a kind of eternal beginning of a thought, a continual opening into a different way of thinking.

"The One Thing That Can Save America" begins with a question about centrality that does not really ever get fully answered.

The second stanza begins as if the poem were going to continue in that direction:

> These are connected to my version of America
> But the juice is elsewhere.
> This morning as I walked out of your room
> After breakfast crosshatched with
> Backward and forward glances, backward into light,
> Forward into unfamiliar light,
> Was it our doing, and was it
> The material, the lumber of life, or of lives
> We were measuring, counting?
> A mood soon to be forgotten
> In crossed girders of light, cool downtown shadow
> In this morning that has seized us again?

The first line feels summative, as if he is about to explain something about the disparate impressions of the first stanza, and to connect them into a larger structure: "These are connected to my version of America." But the poem veers off into a different, more private direction. Again, I think this is precisely what people can find frustrating about Ashbery, and about poetry in general: just when it seems as if it is going to collect into a larger point, a unifying idea, it refuses to. Some people read poems, feel this way, and think they do not know enough about poetry; others resent poetry for not behaving like other forms of writing.

As this second stanza progresses, it becomes clear that the speaker is remembering the morning, getting up, walking out of the lover's room, having had sort of an awkward breakfast "crosshatched with / Backward and forward glances," and then, it seems, wondering how important all this is. Is it "The material, the lumber of life"? Or just "A mood soon to be forgotten," once they are back outside, in the city?

Now the poem is quite personal, maybe even a kind of love poem. Each time I read it, the line "the juice is elsewhere" mystifies me for a moment. It never fails to seem goofy and unexpected. Because of what comes right before it—"These are connected to my version of America"—the line seems related to the discussion of America, as if what the narrator is saying is, "I have thoughts about America, but what is important—the 'juice'—is not in those thoughts, it is elsewhere." Juice is a metaphor for something important, or maybe for electricity or energy.

But there is an equally important literal and mundane meaning we come to understand only retroactively, once we hear the word "breakfast." Actual juice is in another room, and the speaker wants to go in that room to drink it. That humble line, "the juice is elsewhere," is a pivot that takes us from the public and metaphoric realm into what is private, and personal. And the effect of that moment depends on our common understanding of that simple word, "juice," which is both what it is and something greater.

The philosopher, writer, and literary critic George Steiner defines every speech act between two people as a kind of translation, a negotiation between what he calls "the external vulgate and the private mass of language." Poetry is the place where the ultimately irresolvable negotiation between public and private in language, and in life, is brought forward, to be happily mourned and mournfully celebrated.

Somehow, when I first read this poem, in my very baby poet brain I got the message that in poetry, just as happens constantly in our own minds, the biggest kinds of thoughts about life and the world can shift with ease into very personal and intimate ones, and back again. To achieve these shifts in writing poetry, with grace and good humor and ease, is a very difficult thing indeed, one that takes a long time to learn to do.

THE POEM BEGAN BY BRINGING UP THE QUESTION OF CENTRAL- ity. Without the title, we wouldn't necessarily connect this poem with a larger, American problem. The title situates us, and con- textualizes the first question about centrality, making it about America, and whatever can save it. As we have seen, the begin- ning of the second stanza—"These are connected to my version of America"—reminds us that this poem is concerned with civic life, among other things. The poem then takes a turn away from these larger, civic issues as the third stanza begins to blend these private and public worlds.

> I know that I braid too much my own
> Snapped-off perceptions of things as they come to me.
> They are private and always will be.
> Where then are the private turns of event
> Destined to bloom later like golden chimes
> Released over a city from a highest tower?
> The quirky things that happen to me, and I tell you,
> And you instantly know what I mean?
> What remote orchard reached by winding roads
> Hides them? Where are these roots?

He feels isolated by his own strangeness, in a way that might feel familiar to many of us. No matter how much we talk and try to communicate, the desire to be understood, to tell someone "the quirky things that happen to me" and for that someone to "instantly know what I mean," can never be fully realized. He acknowledges with honest resignation that these "Snapped-off perceptions" are private and always will be. The melancholy produced by that knowledge suffuses the poem.

I think if we are being honest, we probably would admit that at times we fear there is an unbridgeable gap between us and others—readers, friends, family, partners—that language cannot cross. Or maybe we fear the gap is in fact bridgeable by someone less damaged or more talented or attractive or authentic than ourselves. To cross this gap is the dream of all writers, and that dream is a kind of metonymy of the human dream to cross over into intimacy or connection. It is this melancholy awareness of inevitable distance between humans, and the hope that it can somehow be crossed over, that gently permeates this poem.

I know that even now, after all these years, I still feel what Ashbery writes to be close to my disappointments and pleasures and hopes in literature and life. I too feel that "I braid too much my own / Snapped off perceptions of things as they come to me." And I wonder and worry now, as I did then and probably always have, about the connection between my private thoughts and life, and the world and people surrounding me. And I feel great joy at moments of connection with others, probably because I have come to see how provisional and hard-won they are.

In this poem, the question is not just private, but public too. The necessary and impossible imperative to reconcile the individual, private consciousness with other people is, it turns out, just like the problem of democracy itself. The tension of centrality—an authority we need to bind us together, and a resistance to that authority—is the fundamental American paradox. How can we come together in a collective, of individuals, of ethnic groups, of states, and maintain our freedom and individuality? It's messy and probably impossible. The constant tension we feel in the American experiment is because of this irreconcilable, and necessary, state of contradiction. It occurs to me it is not a stretch to call America the negative capability country, though so often we do not feel capable at all of being in mysteries, uncertainties, doubts, without an irritable reaching after fact or reason, a desire for centrality, for everything to be once and for all resolved.

This poem moves back and forth between thinking, albeit obliquely, about the contradictions in our public and civic structures, and thinking about the same conflicts as they arise in a private life. What happens when my private desires need to be reconciled with the larger world? It is the question anyone concerned about individuality, but also about others, about connection, must ask. And it is the question anyone who is interested in union of any kind—private or public—must keep asking. It is the great question of democracy, the irresolvable, quintessentially American question, and in asking it, the poem is quintessentially American too.

"THE ONE THING THAT CAN SAVE AMERICA" ENDS BY MOVING away from the "I" of the previous stanza, and returning to the pronoun "we," as well as the indeterminate "you." The predicament of the end of the poem is therefore simultaneously collective, and also still private and personal:

> It is the lumps and trials
> That tell us whether we shall be known
> And whether our fate can be exemplary, like a star.
> All the rest is waiting
> For a letter that never arrives,
> Day after day, the exasperation
> Until finally you have ripped it open not knowing what it is,
> The two envelope halves lying on a plate.
> The message was wise, and seemingly

Dictated a long time ago.
Its truth is timeless, but its time has still
Not arrived, telling of danger, and the mostly limited
Steps that can be taken against danger
Now and in the future, in cool yards,
In quiet small houses in the country,
Our country, in fenced areas, in cool shady streets.

Part of life is the hard experiences that are themselves some-
how the signs of living a worthwhile life, "the lumps and trials"
that will somehow "tell us whether we shall be known / And
whether our fate can be exemplary, like a star." But the other part
of life is just "waiting." "All the rest is waiting."

The letter never arrives but also somehow in the end it does,
and you rip it open with impatience, though you have no idea what
is inside. And the letter is both relevant to what is going on now
and also not yet relevant: "Its truth is timeless, but its time has still
/ Not arrived, telling of danger, and the mostly limited / Steps
that can be taken against danger." I think of this impossible letter
that both does and does not arrive, with its futile and vital advice,
as very much like a poem. Or maybe even more like the elusive
truth of a poem, which is less like a final answer or outcome we are
supposed to "get," and more like a position of open, questioning
alertness that the poem is designed to produce.

Right at the end, Ashbery writes, "In quiet small houses in the
country," and then, in the last line, corrects himself: actually it is
"Our country," and once again the poem is not just about a private
moment for one particular consciousness, but our collective fears
and dreams and desires.

The lovely, melancholic irony of this poem is that in exploring
and acknowledging the impossibility of reconciling the public and

the private, the poem brings us together. The poet, in being authentic to a private way of thinking, creates a space that others can enter. The reader is both with the poet, and also still alone.

There are no big solutions coming. This is disappointing and troubling. It is maybe also a relief. "The poem is sad, because it wants to be yours, and cannot." In that very sadness, conjured by the poem, there is companionship, a shared recognition. Or, as Wallace Stevens writes at the end of one of his last poems, "Final Soliloquy of the Interior Paramour," in reading poetry together "We make a dwelling in the evening air, / In which being there together is enough."

"The One Thing That Can Save America" implicitly asserts the value of a different way of thinking about big ideas, one that rejects centrality without retreating entirely into esoteric privacy. The poem is an embodiment of the contradiction between the inner and outer worlds. The poem also reminds us of the dual nature of language, how each word means something particular to a person, and how we are also somehow not locked into those personal associations. We are able to understand each other, to somehow, magically and mysteriously, move out of the private mass of language and into the external vulgate, a public space of communication, to talk to each other.

The poem also presents a kind of knowledge that is not mere information. The poem might even be quietly declaring itself to be the final repository, at least in language, of this kind of experience. The one thing that can save America is this poem. Maybe in its willingness to gently correct itself. Or in the dreamlike yet waking state it can create in us, that cautious, mysterious force from within, that gives us a space to think more freely, for at least a few moments. The true meaning of a poem isn't hidden in a textbook, or in the mind of a teacher, or expert, or even the poet who wrote it. It comes to be, each time, in the mind of each half-dreaming reader.

"THE ONE THING THAT CAN SAVE AMERICA" HELPS ME LIVE MY life, both as a private and public citizen. In a gentle, nonprescriptive, and associative way, it thinks about the difference between the public and private spheres. It driftingly and unsystematically brings up a feeling of distance between an individual consciousness and a public one. It asserts that what we most need to discover, "the mostly limited / Steps that can be taken against danger," are in a letter that will never arrive.

And somehow, every time I read this poem, I feel the letter has arrived, that I do understand, that I am not doomed to eternal privacy, that I have company in my thoughts. The poem also helps me live my life by reminding me that there is a possibility of a different way of thinking, and that I am not alone in my desire for it.

At the end of "The Noble Rider and the Sound of Words," Stevens explains what he means by nobility. For him it is an elusive quality located in thought and language, one for which poets search. Nobility is something much more than mere style or superficial poeticizing, what Stevens calls the "lifeless nobility" of rhetoric and mere fine words. He writes, "There is no element more conspicuously absent from contemporary poetry . . . no element that poets have sought after, more curiously and more piously, certain of its obscure existence."

According to Stevens, and I think he is right, this quality of nobility has nothing to do with a particular style of poetry. Styles of poetry change with and reflect the times. This happens again and again in the history of literature and art. But regardless of their external qualities and forms, true poems carry within them this ineffable, timeless quality of nobility: "But as a wave is a force and not the water of which it is composed, which is never the same, so nobility is a force and not the manifestations of which it is composed, which are never the same."

Stevens then goes on to describe this nobility, so rare and so essential to poetry and to life, in what might at first seem to be curious terms:

> *It is a violence from within that protects us from a violence without. It is the imagination pressing back against the pressure of reality. It seems, in the last analysis, to have something to do with our self-preservation; and that, no doubt, is why the expression of it, the sound of its words, helps us to live our lives.*

Stevens is arguing for the need, at times, to actively resist the pressure of all the news and information and input with which we are flooded, to push back with force to create a different kind of space within ourselves. To do so is not to bury our heads and ignore what is going on around us. Stevens writes of modern poetry, "It has to think about war / And it has to find what will suffice." To resist the pressure of the real is to preserve a space within ourselves, where everything we see and know can get recombined, in the hopes of a deeper and more mysterious knowledge. We do this resisting, this pushing back, not with the euphemism or the rhetoric of politics, nor with the received dead language of any ideology, but with words alive with possibility, charged with meaning. It is as if what Stevens is proposing is a kind of environmentalism of the imagination, a call for us to actively carve out in our own minds and daily lives a space for imagination that is like a nature preserve or ecologically protected area.

More and more, as a result of technology, we are experiencing our own minds in different, faster, more scattered ways. The pervasive, immediate availability of information is a relatively recent phenomenon. Now, for so many of us in the developed world, as soon as the feeling starts to come upon us that we do not know something, immediately also comes the almost overwhelming urge, one which can usually be instantly gratified, to look it up "in the cloud," to find the answer. At times, I am sure it is good to know as much as we can about the world. At others, I feel quite sure almost all of this knowledge is extraneous, even anesthetizing. When it comes to social issues, the ease with which we can find out information and vicariously experience the suffering of others can make us feel as if, merely by knowing something and passing it along, we are *doing* something, when in fact, sadly, we are not.

When Stevens writes that the role of the poet is to help people live their lives, it sounds very grandiose. But really what he means is that the role of the poet as he perceives it is to deepen experience, to write poems that we can use to protect ourselves in some small way against the constant encroachment of "the pressure of the real," the mundane, terrifying, distracting, and often monetary, pressures that can make us feel like automatons. The original Surrealists of the 1930s in France had a similar, utopian, impossible desire for poetry, that it would reconnect our daily existence with the world of imagination and dreams that modern life has split from us, leaving us in constant deadening pain.

This resistance we find through reading a poem like "The One Thing That Can Save America" or any other does not take the place of knowledge or action. We desperately need information, and stories, and the news, and essays and everything else, not just for the information they give us, but, even more important, for the experience of being with a mind thinking clearly, understanding the world so that we can better understand it too. But we also desperately need poetry, for something else.

W. S. Merwin said, "Poetry addresses individuals in their most intimate, private, frightened and elated moments. People turn to poetry in times of crisis because it comes closer than any other art form to addressing what cannot be said. In expressing the inexpressible poetry remains close to the origins of language." Poet and activist Brenda Hillman said that a poem "makes something out of a moment of consciousness that couldn't be said any other way."

There are many things we need to say and think that we almost cannot. These vital things approach, without ever attaining, the inexpressible. Poetry pushes away some of our usual ways of using language, of thinking, in order to lead us up to those moments together, so in the moment of reading, and perhaps right after, we can feel and know something we otherwise could not. Reading or listening to poems is such a different experience from the rest of our lives. The more we are colonized by our devices and the "information" and "experiences" that they supposedly deliver, the more we need a true experience of unmonetized attention.

William Carlos Williams famously wrote, "It is difficult / to get the news from poems / yet men die miserably every day / for lack of what is found there." The "news" of poetry is something more than mere information, facts and opinions. When I think about the word "news," I am reminded that the word "gospel" comes from the Greek word "*euangelion*," "good news." The good news of poetry is not that everything is going to be okay, or that we don't have to worry, or that we can retreat to our imaginations while the world burns. On the contrary. The news is that there is always a place where, for a few moments at least, we can feel protected against the constant superficial, distracting noise that is the pressure of the real, where we can feel renewed, so that something else can begin to happen.

7

NEGATIVE CAPABILITY

WHEN I BEGAN TO UNDERSTAND THAT POETRY WAS GOING TO BE central to my life, it was thrilling, but also confusing and difficult, in that way things can be for someone who is twenty-four. I had thought I was going to be an academic, or maybe a lawyer like my dad. So I felt constantly, pervasively ambivalent and unsure. I also felt like I should already *know* what I should be doing with my life, and that gap between what I knew and what I thought I should greatly troubled me. I sense a similar troubled feeling in so many of my students, and want somehow to reassure them, though I know this is impossible.

Eventually I decided the only way forward for me as a poet was to liberate myself from the scholarly path I had set myself on, and to pursue writing poetry full-time, whatever that would mean. I had known exactly one person who had gone to an MFA program in creative writing, so I thought I would apply for one of those too. I knew hardly anything about them but it seemed like the best way forward.

So in my second year at Berkeley, I studied for my master's exams in Slavic languages and literatures, which you had to pass to go on to the doctoral program. The exams included an oral component conducted in Russian, and required mastery of an immense reading list. So at the beginning of that summer before my second year, I made a schedule, which involved basically reading from eight in the morning until midnight, with breaks only to teach and eat and occasionally play a little basketball. I was also trying to write as many poems as I could, and getting my applications for creative writing programs together. I wasn't sure I was going to leave yet, or really of anything.

The exams were quite brutal, but I passed. And I got into some MFA programs too, including the one at the University of Massachusetts at Amherst, just down the road from where I had gone to college. I felt excited and unsure and confused. I still felt very uncertain as to whether I was making the right decision, leaving academia, which at least felt safe, for the crazy venture of starting to become a poet.

I finally made the decision to leave and go to Amherst for my MFA. Soon after, I was summoned to an exit interview with the very stern head of my department. She was an exceptionally intimidating Russian scholar of modernism, semiotics, and, more recently, cultural and literary conceptions of suicide. Mostly I listened while she told me that since I had done well on the exams, I was welcome to come back to Berkeley as soon as I was done with poetry. But I should know that in order to be an academic, I would have to stop jumping around all the time from one idea to another to another, and settle on one "worldview," that would provide the consistency that would allow me to produce academic work. In other words, I should get this jumping around out of my system before I returned.

During that year, I had come across John Keats's well-known (at least among poets) letter of December 1817, in which he writes to his brothers:

> . . . *and at once it struck me what quality went to form a Man of Achievement, especially in Literature, and which Shakespeare possessed so enormously—I mean Negative Capability, that is, when a man is capable of being in uncertainties, mysteries, doubts, without any irritable reaching after fact and reason.*

When I first read Keats's letter, because I didn't know any other poets, and was just starting to really learn about poetry, I thought negative capability was some obscure concept I had personally unearthed. I talked incessantly about it to my peers in the PhD program, as the key to understanding literature, not to mention life.

Reading Keats's words above was practically a shock to my system. It was intensely liberating as a writer to realize that the poem is not a place to be categorically convinced of anything. It is a good place to be serially convinced, convinced for a moment, in a line or a stanza or a phrase or even a word. But then to change one's mind. Again and again. And it was intensely liberating as well, if quite terrifying, to begin to realize that I was going to devote my life to searching for this feeling in writing.

According to Keats, the poem is also a place to remain in what he calls a bit later in the letter "half knowledge." Somewhere between not knowing and full knowledge there is an intermediate, contradictory state of half knowledge (what we could also call reverie, drifting, or lucid dreaming), where one goes in order to write poetry, and when one reads it.

Listening to my brilliant department chair, I had a rare moment of clarity. I realized she was absolutely right about my tendency to jump around, and that this was exactly why I would never be a good scholar. For better, and worse, I instinctively wanted half knowledge, which would lead to a different sort of truth that I could not find anywhere else but in poetry.

KEATS, WITH THE PARTICULAR CRUELTY OF A YOUNG POET, holds up the brilliant, erratic, tormented Coleridge as an example of a poet who was unable to sustain negative capability: "Coleridge, for instance, would let go by a fine isolated verisimilitude caught from the Penetralium of mystery, from being incapable of remaining content with half knowledge. This pursued through Volumes would perhaps take us no further than this, that with a great poet the sense of Beauty overcomes every other consideration, or rather obliterates all consideration."

For Keats, Coleridge is not a great poet because he fails to see that settling for "half knowledge" is, in poetry at least, not a failure, but a requirement. When I left a scholarly life for a poetic one, I found this idea both sustaining and frightening. I knew somehow that pushing away the anxious need to be right, or smart, or consistent, or accurate, in favor of a more intuitive and partial and therefore potentially more beautiful type of knowledge, was related to writing poetry. But I did not know how to get there.

A verisimilitude is something that gives the appearance of truth. In life, this can be problematic: we might be fooled by something that seems true, or lifelike, but is not.

Poetry, however, makes its meaning through a series of verisimilitudes. Each moment in the poem seems at the moment completely real or true, regardless of what has come before or after. This is what negative capability means in poetry, to be in the state where you can accept a succession of things, especially if they contradict each other, in order to allow within yourself an experience that you will not have elsewhere in life.

It's no coincidence that Keats's ideas about negative capability in his letter come as he is thinking about Shakespeare. Shakespeare's plays were a lifetime preoccupation for Keats. We know from his letters that he read them practically religiously, and used them as an ongoing inspiration.

Shakespeare's plays are, as we know, populated by some of the most vivid characters ever created. They feel alive to us. When we read them, or see and hear them onstage, we experience each of these characters as fully developed beings, with ways of seeing the world that are, for them when they are speaking, fully true. We know these points of view are inherently limited, but that does not make them any less real. These limitations are precisely what make the characters feel so alive.

The perspectives of the characters conflict, giving the plays their plots and energies. It's not that we necessarily agree with the characters, or approve of their actions, especially some of the most vivid—Lear, Othello, Iago, Macbeth, and so on—who are the agents of their own disasters. It's possible to know a character is mistaken, but also to become completely immersed in his or her point of view, especially during a soliloquy.

Keats's great insight was that the moments of a poem function the way that a Shakespeare play does. A poem does not exist in order to get a single message across, or to privilege one idea above all others. The poem places us in a state of heightened importance, with a sense that everything matters intensely at the moment it is being experienced. Like the plays, what gives a great poem energy is the movement from one moment to the next, each moment a place to be convinced, regardless of whether it is consistent with what has come before.

IN DECEMBER 1817, WHEN KEATS WROTE THIS LETTER, HE WAS only twenty-two years old. But he was also less than a year and a half from the spring of 1819, when he would begin to write his great odes, which are among the greatest ever written in the English language. And not quite two years after that spring, on February 23, 1821, he would die at the age of twenty-five of tuberculosis in Rome, in a small apartment at 26 Piazza Spagna, right next to the Spanish Steps. The bedroom there is still preserved as it was when he died, and it's a solemn place to make a little visit.

In "Ode on a Grecian Urn" Keats writes many things that are, strictly speaking, not easy to reconcile with each other. The overall structure of the poem is clear: the speaker is looking at an urn, and what is depicted on it, and thinking about a lot of things in relation to what he is seeing. Here is the first stanza:

> Thou still unravish'd bride of quietness,
>> Thou foster-child of silence and slow time,
> Sylvan historian, who canst thus express
>> A flowery tale more sweetly than our rhyme:
> What leaf-fring'd legend haunts about thy shape
>> Of deities or mortals, or of both,
>>> In Tempe or the dales of Arcady?
>> What men or gods are these? What maidens loth?
> What mad pursuit? What struggle to escape?
>>> What pipes and timbrels? What wild ecstasy?

The "thou," or you, in the poem is the urn: the speaker is talking to it. The urn is married to quietness, though the two have

not yet consummated their relationship. It's also an orphan, a fos-
ter child adopted by a couple my wife and I would feel quite okay
about going on vacation with: silence and slow time. The poet is
looking at the figures on the urn: "legend" in this case seems to re-
fer to a less common definition of that word, which is an inscription
on an object. The poet can't read the legend, the words on the urn.
Maybe he doesn't speak Greek. So he has to wonder.

The poet also wonders, what is going on with these figures
depicted on the urn? Are they gods, or mortals, or both mixed
together? Someone is chasing someone endlessly. The poet looks
with great care at every detail of the urn, falling deeper into the
spell of its mysterious landscape, continuing to ask questions he
cannot answer. The whole rest of the poem is driven by the en-
ergy of this not-knowing. The poem is an experience of continual
speculation and wondering.

There is also a lot of contradiction in the poem. Right after the
poet gets finished telling us that the urn is both a bride and a child
of silence, he calls it a "sylvan historian," a historian of the woods,
one that expresses "a flowery tale." That the offspring of silence
would talk is, if not exactly a contradiction, at least unexpected.

If in reading the poem you get distracted by an irritable need
to come up with a consistent, coherent set of ideas that the speaker
has in his feelings about the urn, an overall message about the
urn, or silence, or time, or mortality, instead of thinking about the
statements of the poem as a series of deeply felt, shifting, even con-
tradictory thoughts, you will miss what is truly great about the
experience of reading it. Maybe poems are not to be read for their
great answers, but for their great, more often than not unanswer-
able, questions.

Unlike every other use of language, poems are where contra-
dictions and possibilities of the material of our meaning-making

system are not an unfortunate and troubling ghost in the machine: they are brought forth to be celebrated. The role of the poem is to bring out *all* the aspects of language: its provisionality, uncertainty, slippage, as well as its miraculous ability to communicate, to mean. Consistency, logic, the pleasurable obligations of plot and setting and characters . . . those are conveniences for the poet, to be adopted or discarded at will. What are the marks of a failed language act everywhere else—not following through on what you have started to say, jumping around and making unjustified connections, saying what is beautiful and exciting rather than what is strictly necessary, and so on—are, if not the mark of, at least the beginnings of poetry.

The ultimate moment of negative capability occurs at the very end of the poem. " 'Beauty is truth, truth beauty,—that is all / Ye know on earth, and all ye need to know,' " says the urn. It is the urn itself that is speaking, something which I forget each time, probably because I have been told by Keats at the beginning that the urn is a kind of avatar of silence! Like so many of the other statements in the poem, this final one is a passionately expressed truth that is only partially true. At this moment, at the end of this poem, for the poet beauty and truth are the same. Yet strictly speaking, of course, this is not true. Even if *sometimes* it is true, it is definitely not *all* you know on earth, nor all you *need* to know!

But every single time I read the poem, in that moment I feel totally convinced. Not because of logic, or even because I have faith. That moment in the poem is a final reaction to the experience of seeing the urn, and meditating upon it. In that moment, the speaker in that poem feels sure that this is the most important truth there is, and for those of us who make a deep connection with the poem, each time we read those lines we feel that is true, in that moment, too. Only when I read the poem and experience it as its thinking unfolds do I feel sure the urn is right, and I go back to reading the poem from start to finish in great part to feel that way again, when in the rest of life I most often cannot.

Instead of objecting to, or trying to reconcile with a single overarching interpretation, the contradictions or lack of an overall coherence of thought in a poem, it is best to embrace that strangeness, to think about what questions it raises, and to let those questions lead us to the deeper thinking the poem exists to produce. When we read a poem, if it is doing what it is supposed to do, we are not "irritably reaching after fact or reason," or some overall view of the world that will settle for once and for all the questions raised by the poem. We experience each moment in the poem as authentic and true. And the overall effect of this experience is to put us, as Valéry writes, in the poetic state of mind.

The poem places us in the middle of the inherently contradictory nature of being. While reading the poem, it is possible for us to be in touch with a deeper truth. Negative capability is just one way of describing this feeling, of being in a place of possibility and freedom that is intimately related to the slippery, provisional, wondrously meaningful nature of language itself.

MOST SERIOUS READERS OF POETRY REALIZE SOONER OR LATER that it is far too limiting to look for a single meaning in a poem. There can, however, be an overreaction to this realization, an idea that poems don't really mean anything specific at all, that they are totally subjective and ambiguous, and whatever the reader gets out of them is just fine.

Teachers of poetry in particular are all too familiar with this vexing idea. Students, once they understand that there is no rigid single meaning to a work of art or piece of writing, often react violently in the other direction, insisting on a total subjectivity that can border on nihilism. This can be quite frustrating, especially when students insist on their prerogatives to completely misread a poem, ignoring the words that are on the page in favor of some interpretation for which there is little or no actual linguistic evidence.

In *Seven Types of Ambiguity* the critic William Empson attempted to explore the nature of ambiguity, and its relationship to meaning. Empson was well aware of how literature explores the potential for multiple meanings in language. And he was equally aware of the likelihood that writers and readers would misunderstand the nature of this ambiguity:

> *[Ambiguity] is not to be respected in so far as it is due to weakness or thinness of thought, obscures the matter at hand unnecessarily . . . or when the interest of the passage is not focussed upon it, so that it is merely an opportunism in the handling of the material, if the reader will not understand the ideas which are being shuffled, and will be given a general impression of incoherence.*

A failure to read carefully, or a projection of whatever comes to mind onto the text: this type of ambiguity, incoherent and weak, is not Empson's. Nor is it the "uncertainties, mysteries, doubts" of Keats's negative capability: as anyone who has read Keats's letters or poetry can see, his idea of the reading experience is a series of passionate, committed attachments, as far as possible from a free-floating, provisional, easily changeable ambiguity.

In the face of this insistence on a certain kind of ambiguity, it is completely understandable, though unfortunate, that teachers would settle on a basic "theme" or "meaning" of the poem in order to corral all these wild and inaccurate speculations. It's a hard problem teachers have, to get students to accept a poem's elusive potentialities for mystery and order and anarchy.

It is also inevitable that the more someone feels connected to a poem, the more likely the poem is to make that person feel compelled to drift into their own experiences and ideas. If the mechanism of the poem is working for a reader, it will have an effect on the reader's mind after the poem is done. The machine of the poem will continue working in the mind of each reader.

The problem with so much discussion of what poems "mean" is that this very natural continuing associative process is either cauterized (it's not "part of the poem" so you can't talk about it), or forced back into the interpretation of the poem itself, which explains why teachers are so often mystified by why a student says a poem is "about" something when clearly it is not. There needs to be a place in talking about poetry for these private thoughts to occur.

I have through trial and error discovered it is a good idea to mark a border, between on the one hand what the poem is actually saying and suggesting, in its words on the page, and on the other what it makes each of us as readers think of for ourselves. The former can be a subject of collective discussion: who is speaking, where are they talking, how are the objects and ideas and occurrences in the poem interacting, and so on. Sometimes it takes a little while to work these things out, and it helps to talk about them all together in a classroom. The latter, those private associations particular to each reader, can be valued too, maybe in a journal or some other space that protects the intimacies of personal experience and imagination.

KEATS'S ODE "TO AUTUMN" IS WRITTEN IN DIRECT ADDRESS "to" that season, personified as the "gleaner" with his hook, a being very much like the familiar figure of Death. In the third and final stanza, everything thrums with significance. There is no content or message to the poem more important than the terrifying and awesome awareness of mortality the poem somehow nearly two centuries later still can conjure.

The speaker in the poem thinks of the songs of spring, and celebrates the music of autumn. Clouds, gnats, swallows, lambs, crickets, the robin in the garden: they are all making noise. There is no "message" other than the fact of the collective song their noises make, and what the speaker creates out of addressing the season, autumn:

> Where are the songs of Spring? Ay, where are they?
>   Think not of them, thou hast thy music too,—
> While barred clouds bloom the soft-dying day,
>   And touch the stubble-plains with rosy hue;
> Then in a wailful choir the small gnats mourn
>   Among the river swallows, borne aloft
>   Or sinking as the light wind lives or dies;
> And full-grown lambs loud bleat from hilly bourn;
>   Hedge-crickets sing; and now with treble soft
> The redbreast whistles from a garden-croft,
>   And gathering swallows twitter in the skies.

The delicate work of bringing us to such moments of awareness is the true work of poetry. This is why "about" is such a counterproductive term in relation to poetry (as unproductive as "looks like" for a painting, as if the sole purpose of a painting were to re-present the world). What is the poem "about"? This question inevitably carries within it the implicit message that the poem is a beautiful (at best) container for something more essential than the experience of reading it. Really, when a poem is functioning, it could best be said to be "about" "aboutness"—that is, "about" the wordless moment we can only be brought to through words, when we perceive the contradictory yet also harmonious significance of everything.

To say a poem is about "aboutness" is not to say it is meaning-less. Meaning-making is always, gloriously, a part of the language act, and meaning-making is therefore an essential part of the poetic act. It is not just the sounds but the actual meaning of the words of a prayer that can bring the religious closer to the presence of the word-less divine. Likewise readers of poetry are brought to the wordless moment—the unsayable, or the poetic state of mind—through a process in which words and their meanings unfold, in time.

The importance of the moment of perception itself, or aware-ness, an awakening to a feeling that something meaningful is happening, can often be the climactic moment of a poem. In the sec-ond stanza of Ashbery's "As You Came from the Holy Land," the speaker in the poem is watching someone sitting and reading, "not wanting to be disturbed." It is the end of summer ("a note of panic in the late August air"), and the speaker starts to hear something, as if the landscape itself and all its elements had begun to speak:

> what lethargy in the avenues
> where all is said in a whisper
> what tone of voice among the hedges
> what tone under the apple trees
> the numbered land stretches away
> and your house is built in tomorrow
> but surely not before the examination
> of what is right and will befall
> not before the census
> and the writing down of names

The poem continues, as a sense of time onrushing inexorably forward creates a sense in the speaker of great portentousness:

the time is ripe now and the adage
is hatching as the seasons change and tremble
it is finally as though that thing of monstrous interest
were happening in the sky
but the sun is setting and prevents you from seeing it.

What is important here is not the cause of the feeling, but the feeling itself. It cannot be known by the speaker what exactly is producing this feeling, what the "it" is in "it is finally as though." That last image, of the "thing of monstrous interest," is so striking that it is easy to forget that this is a long metaphor. Whatever is happening, whatever the speaker is feeling, feels *as if* "that thing of monstrous interest / were happening in the sky."

It is never specified what, exactly, is producing these feelings. Maybe it's an actual event, like the end of a love affair or friendship. Or perhaps it's simply the time of year, or some unnameable sense of anxiety or dread.

Haven't we all had those moments of deep inexplicable feeling, of sadness or melancholy or joy that we can't quite place? Maybe we don't often share those moments because in order to, we would have to try to say why we feel they are important, which would mean distilling them down in a way that does not feel accurate to the entirety of the process of understanding. Or maybe it's only possible to have those feelings when one is truly alone.

8

THREE POLITICAL POEMS

IT IS A POWERFUL THING WHEN A POEM FINDS ITS WAY, DI-rectly or otherwise, to the biggest issues in our social lives. Yet even the greatest poets can stumble when they start to bend their poems to a political purpose. Political poems have a tendency to turn into lyricized essays, or editorials, or sermons, or rants. This is partially because the language of politics is so often designed to do the opposite of what poems do: the poet has to remain vigilant not to slip into euphemism, generalization, obscuring abstraction. And it is also because the subject matter is so important to the poet, which can cause the poet to begin to prioritize tasks better left to prose: informing, convincing, lecturing, describing, reporting. When that happens, the poems, however laudable in their inten-tions, can stop feeling like poems, and become more like, at best, poetic prose, and at worst, decorative, unnecessary lyricizing.

One of the most useful descriptions of this danger is in Richard Hugo's little manual about writing poetry, *The Triggering Town*. Hugo talks bluntly to beginning poets about a choice they have in relation to language. Are they going to try to control it, to make it say what they want it to say? Or are they going to follow its possibilities, even (and maybe even especially) if those possibilities lead them away from their original intentions?

This, according to Hugo, is the inescapable choice only poetry requires us to make. Here he makes a distinction between poetry as a genre and other genres such as journalism:

> *In the news article the relation of the words to the subject . . . is a strong one. The relation of the words to the writer is so weak that for our purposes it isn't worth consideration. Since the majority of your reading has been newspapers, you are used to seeing language function this way.*
>
> *That's how prose works. When writing it, we ultimately always care about using language to do something. Poetry, on the other hand, requires us to rethink our instinctive hierarchy of content over the material of language:*
>
> *When you write a poem these relations must reverse themselves. That is, the relation of the words to the subject must weaken and the relation of the words to the writer (you) must take on strength. . . . This is probably the hardest thing about writing poems. It may be a problem with every poem, at least for a long time. Somehow you must switch your allegiance from the triggering subject to the words.*

So many times I have taught this essay by Hugo, and every single time, my students immediately start to worry. What about what I *want* to say, about my personal experiences, or about the

world? Shouldn't I be expressing myself and my ideas through po-
etry? Are you saying that we should write poetry that isn't true,
or relevant to the big problems of the world? What about what is
right, and good? I tell them to keep reading, as Hugo anticipates
this objection:

> *By now you may be thinking, doesn't this lead finally to*
> *amoral and shallow writing? Yes it does, if you are amoral*
> *and shallow. I hope it will lead you to yourself and the way*
> *you feel. All poets I know, and I know plenty of them, have*
> *an unusually strong moral sense, and that is why they can*
> *go into the cynical world of the imagination and not feel so*
> *threatened that they become impotent. There's fear sometimes*
> *involved but also joy, an exhilaration that can't be explained*
> *to anyone who has not experienced it. Don't worry about*
> *morality. Most people who worry about morality ought to.*

For Hugo, following the suggestions of the material of lan-
guage, instead of trying to bend it to expressing what we already
know, is inherently ethical. Following our internal sense of music
leads to us revealing who we really are. Keats thought this too.
In his negative capability letter, he writes that "with a great poet
the sense of Beauty overcomes every other consideration, or rather
obliterates all consideration."

"Beauty," here, is an easily misunderstood term. It is so easily
confused with mere decoration, art that doesn't have a commitment
to deep meaning, art that merely diverts, as opposed to engaging
with the great problems of the world. But Keats isn't making an ar-
gument that poems should be merely decorative or pretty. His great
odes are the furthest things from mere aesthetic exercises. They are
mortally engaged with the deepest concerns of any living person.

In poetry, beauty can be far more than mere prettiness, though it is good that for some poets that is enough. For some poets, a sense of beauty will be in sound, or in the visual images language can conjure. For others it will be in the disruption a poem can create. And for still others, the beauty of a poem will have far less to do with what we ordinarily consider beautiful or "poetic" language, and far more to do with the powerful, striking movement of the mind as it thinks through complex or difficult issues, personal or political or environmental or global. These poems can take on a role of advocacy or polemic, while also remaining inside the unsolvability of it all.

Poets are at their best when they follow Keats's and Hugo's advice, to see where the language leads them, and where they as poets end up when they follow it. What is on our minds, what we care about most, we find a way to talk about. If you are a person who really, truly cares about the environment or politics or equality in matters of race or gender or economics or anywhere else, these concerns will naturally emerge in your poems. Your only job is to follow your instinctive, personal, idiosyncratic sense of what is beautiful, and to see what emerges. The danger of course is that in doing so you are likely to discover and reveal what it is you really care about.

THE GREATEST POEMS WRITTEN ABOUT POLITICAL ISSUES OFTEN contain within them a central ambiguity that competes with genuine certainty and rage. Amiri Baraka's glorious, problematic poem "Somebody Blew Up America" is a poem full of beauty and truth, along with rage and confusion. In it, Baraka for some reason repeats an untrue legend that there were no Jews who died in the World Trade Center attacks. I still can't really understand what he

was trying to do there, whether he was being ironic, or just repeat-
ing a question people had, or if he really believed that.

That one moment in the poem, understandably, has become a
focal point of much discussion. It's definitely a poem that troubles
me personally. But I also love it: its sound and meaning and genu-
ine, desperate, angry questioning feel completely authentic and
necessary to me.

We know who the people are who blew up the World Trade
Center buildings. But who blew up *America*? Who ruined and
destroyed our country, and turned everything that is good into
something awful? According to the title, somebody. The poem is
a kind of increasingly desperate, futile investigation into who that
somebody might be.

This investigation is not primarily logical and rational. It is
not an argument for a coherent way of thinking. It is not even an
answer. It is a series of questions. We find genuine questions ev-
erywhere in poetry because they direct the language away from
certainty and stasis, while also leaving plenty of room to be con-
crete and precise. In the best poems, often the poet does not know
the answers.

Here, the question is, "Who?" Asking it with increasing anger
and despair, the poet turns into a kind of epistemological owl:

> Who make money from war
> Who make dough from fear and lies
> Who want the world like it is
> Who want the world to be ruled by imperialism and national
>   oppression and terror violence, and hunger and poverty.
>
> Who is the ruler of Hell?
> Who is the most powerful

Who you know ever
Seen God?

But everybody seen
The Devil

Like an Owl exploding
In your life in your brain in your self
Like an Owl who know the devil
All night, all day if you listen, Like an Owl
Exploding in fire. We hear the questions rise
In terrible flame like the whistle of a crazy dog

Like the acid vomit of the fire of Hell
Who and Who and WHO who who
Whoooo and Whooooooooooooooooooooooo!

This poem asks, who is responsible for the terrible things that are happening all around us? And the poem is willing to continually rest in half knowledge, to enact the feelings of anger and uncertainty and even the impossibility of knowledge. It is in this willingness that the poem makes its meaning, something far beyond mere polemic. Again and again in this poem "We hear the questions rise / In terrible flame" until the poem ends with the cry "Who" that is both human and animal, extended into a sound that in its very meaninglessness signifies our vast, helpless frustration.

OVER THE PAST SEVERAL YEARS, SINCE I FIRST READ IT, I HAVE come back again and again to "Power," by Audre Lorde, with a mixture of awe and sorrow. Lorde wrote this poem after hearing the news of the acquittal of a white police officer for the killing of a ten-year-old African American boy, in April 1973. The poem begins:

The difference between poetry and rhetoric
is being ready to kill
yourself
instead of your children.

I am trapped on a desert of raw gunshot wounds
and a dead child dragging his shattered black
face off the edge of my sleep
blood from his punctured cheeks and shoulders
is the only liquid for miles
and my stomach
churns at the imagined taste while
my mouth splits into dry lips
without loyalty or reason
thirsting for the wetness of his blood
as it sinks into the whiteness
of the desert where I am lost
without imagery or magic
trying to make power out of hatred and destruction
trying to heal my dying son with kisses
only the sun will bleach his bones quicker.

Right at the beginning of the poem, Lorde is thinking about the danger that her emotions will cause her to forget poetry, and slip into rhetoric, that is, speech designed primarily to argue and to convince. In the first stanza, she seems to refer to Yeats's famous remark "We make out of the quarrels with others, rhetoric, but of the quarrels with ourselves, poetry," while raising the stakes far above mere quarreling, to a mortal level. For her, the issue of *how* to speak about this murder is itself a mortal and moral question.

In the second stanza, she moves into metaphorical territory, using devices we usually think of as poetic, like figurative language and imagery. She intuits that her rage leaves her with no alternative but to become a kind of vampire, "thirsting for the wetness" of the blood of the child. Here, she knows she is locating herself in a territory of great ambiguity, expressing the rage while also standing outside it in fear and wonder.

It is clear that she perceives that her feelings of anger are both justified and also a kind of trap, a continued violence that the very structure of racial violence perpetrates on her. Though there is a logic to it, her knowledge is not primarily logical: it is quick, associative, intuitive, metaphorical, poetic. She conflates the loss of this black child she does not know with the imagined loss of her own son. The poem continues by returning to a more factual and documentary territory:

> A policeman who shot down a ten year old in Queens
> stood over the boy with his cop shoes in childish blood
> and a voice said "Die you little motherfucker" and
> there are tapes to prove it. At his trial
> this policeman said in his own defense
> "I didn't notice the size nor nothing else
> only the color". And
> there are tapes to prove that, too.
>
> Today that 37 year old white man
> with 13 years of police forcing
> was set free
> by eleven white men who said they were satisfied
> justice had been done
> and one Black Woman who said
> "They convinced me" meaning
> they had dragged her 4'10" black Woman's frame
> over the hot coals

of four centuries of white male approval
until she let go
the first real power she ever had
and lined her own womb with cement
to make a graveyard for our children.

Here in the third and fourth stanzas, she is willing to risk leaving behind our traditional conceptions of "poetry" in the interests of directly communicating the facts of the case. It is remarkable here how the initial dilemma of the poem—rhetoric versus poetry—is enacted in the poem itself. These lines might be in a narrow sense more rhetorical and less poetic than the ones earlier in the poem, but they function poetically in the complex ambiguity of the overall structure.

The poem ends with great and dangerous imaginative freedom:

I have not been able to touch the destruction
within me.
But unless I learn to use
the difference between poetry and rhetoric
my power too will run corrupt as poisonous mold
or lie limp and useless as an unconnected wire
and one day I will take my teenaged plug
and connect it to the nearest socket
raping an 85 year old white woman
who is somebody's mother
and as I beat her senseless and set a torch to her bed
a greek chorus will be singing in 3/4 time
"Poor thing. She never hurt a soul. What beasts they are."

It must have taken immense honesty, and both personal and poetic courage, to follow the logic of the poem, to allow herself to imagine that she might plug in her internal adolescent avatar of pure rage, who will then commit an unspeakable act. She reveals something about herself and her rage that is troubling and true. This poem could be seen as a more intuitive and associative version of the explorations in James Baldwin's *Notes of a Native Son*, or Ta-Nehisi Coates's *Between the World and Me*, which explore the internal violence of justified rage. Here, those problems have been made available for us in the starkest and most unrelenting possible manner, while also leaving us in a state of profound and necessary irresolution.

WHENEVER THE ANNIVERSARY OF THE BEGINNING OF OPERAtion Iraqi Freedom comes around again, I remember how, in the months leading up to the invasion, hundreds of thousands of people peaceably moved through the streets of the world's cities. So many were protesting the war, while feeling utterly helpless. The media and government were solemnly discussing in what seemed like reasonable language what was even then clearly an act of insanity.

This always makes me think of a certain poem by W. S. Merwin. "When the War Is Over" appeared in Merwin's classic volume *The Lice*, in 1967 at the height of the Vietnam War.

When the war is over
We will be proud of course the air will be
Good for breathing at last
The waters will have been improved the salmon
And the silence of heaven will migrate more perfectly
The dead will think the living are worth it we will know
Who we are
And we will all enlist again

The war in Merwin's poem comes out of a specific historical context, Vietnam, and would have been read that way at the time. But the poem applies to all wars, in all times.

When, finally, the war is over, "We will be proud of course." This is clearly irony. Everything will work even better than it did before. Isn't that always the noble hope? No one ever *wants* to go to war, we are *forced*, for the betterment of the nation, the world, ourselves, our children, born and unborn. After the war the air and the water will be "improved," as if they need to be, and not just the salmon but even "the silence of heaven" will "migrate more perfectly," as if those things could ever be made more perfect.

"The dead will think the living are worth it." How strange, that the poem asserts such knowledge. The poem is, of course, ironic throughout. Not only is it not possible to know what the dead will think, but it might very well be a dangerous fantasy to insinuate such knowledge is possible at all. In its understated irony the poem is implying we imagine the dead think we the living are "worth it," in order to comfort ourselves, because we have done terrible things or had them done in our names.

This poem is full of simple, direct language and, like many great poems, it is full of ideas. But if "When the War Is Over" is a great political poem, it is not merely because of *what* it says; that is, that our idealized hopes might be the very engine that drives us from one war to the next. Nor that we are all complicit in this collective fantasy. Or even in its irony, the way what it says is measured against what it implies. Those points can all be made in prose. "When the War Is Over" is a great political poem because it rejects all euphemism, reawakens us to what we are actually saying, and brings back our fear of things we should be afraid of. It *places* us in the middle of contradiction, and requires us to accept it. It is an exemplar of negative capability.

Reading "When the War Is Over," it is possible to start to think freely in relation to giant ideas, so casually expressed in the rhetoric that leads up to war, and comes after it. We get a glimmer of the actuality, the paradox and complexity and uncertainty that lie behind that rhetoric. Even the word "war" itself seems to loosen and break free for a moment, so we can experience it in a new way.

It has been said the poet's task is to purify the language of the tribe. That doesn't seem to be what we need right now. Our American language already goes through a daily and brutal process of purification. Certain terms are sanctified and repeated again and again and again until they permeate our consciousness. This mechanism is quite familiar to all of us: for a few days, or maybe a week or two, a certain word or phrase will take over the language of pundits and politicians and make its way down out of our screens and listening devices and then pass through us like some kind of virus. Arab Street. Republican Brand. Public Option. Financial Crisis. Climate Change. Fiscal Cliff. Bailout. Surge. Sequester. Enhanced Interrogation Techniques. Weapons of Mass Destruction. I am fascinated and horrified by this process, especially when I hear those dead metaphors and totally familiarized phrases start to emerge from my own obedient mouth. We don't need a purification of our language, but a reawakening to what we are really saying.

It's easy to be paralyzed into inaction, even nihilism. What difference can my little actions ever have, in the face of global suffering, climate change, vast forces of inequity, horror, and harm? These are the crucial questions of ethics and politics. They can seem impossible to answer. And they can seem even more overwhelming when asked of poetry. I know very few poets who have not, at some time, asked themselves, of what use are my little scratchings in the dust? Especially if I'm not writing "about" the

big issues. Is writing about them the only way to (as Allen Gins-
berg wrote, in "America") put "my queer shoulder to the wheel?"

In our current difficult time, many poems that sincerely at-
tempt to engage the most challenging political, social, and cultural
issues that face us are being written. Most likely only by sustained
poetic attempt can we find the true poetry we need. And, regard-
less of how small and helpless we might feel or even be, one thing
we as individuals *can* always be responsible for is attention to our
language. We can do our best not to let our words delude us into
comfort, and out of whatever actions our souls tell us are compas-
sionate, and therefore correct. This is also what poetry can do to,
and for, and with us. It may not be the solution, but it is at least a
necessary beginning.

9

DREAM MEANING

WE HAVE ALL READ POEMS THAT RHYME, OR THAT HAVE LINE breaks, or that exhibit some other kind of signifier that what we are reading is a poem, and thought to ourselves, there is nothing here. I feel nothing. We feel this nothingness not because we don't know enough about poetry, or because we are missing the key or the code. We feel this way because there is no poetry in this poetry, no movement of the mind that is surprising but also true.

Without some aspect of this type of movement of the mind, something might look like a poem but it won't be. The drifting, associating, linking experience that poetry creates is central to the way it makes meaning.

This associative movement doesn't describe a certain type or subset of poetry. All poetry associates, rhyming conceptually by juxtaposing and connecting ideas that do not ordinarily belong together. Sometimes those associative leaps are flashy and huge (as in Surrealism), at other times, much more subtle. Regardless, poetry by its nature makes meaning by revealing hidden connections.

In various ways, poets look for associations, connections, leaps that feel both surprising and true. Associative movement can manifest in metaphor or other figurative language. It can be in the juxtaposition of facts that do not ordinarily belong together, but that the poem makes seem inevitably related (this may be where the genre of poetry is closest to that of the essay). Or in a leap in the narrative of a poem. Or something musical, like rhyme or some other sound association, that determines the course of the poem above all other consideration. Something that literally or conceptually rhymes or chimes with what has come before.

The more reading I did as I was writing this book, the more I saw the concept of associative movement described in different ways throughout time and across different cultures. Again and again, it is assigned a central place in poetry, beginning with Aristotle in the *Poetics*. His basic definition of a poet is a person who has "an eye for resemblances." This is a way of saying that poets have a talent for seeing latent possible connections in language, what Emerson called the "fossil poetry" in all words, which poets bring back to our awareness again.

Associative movement is not just an English-language or Western phenomenon. In his well-known instructions to poets, *Listen to the Pine*, the great master of haiku Bashō writes about the various ways of linking the stanzas of *haikai no renga* (the longer, collaborative poetic form out of which the three-line haiku emerged): "In the distant past, poets valued lexical links. In the more recent past, poets have stressed content links. Today, it is best to link by transference, reverberation, scent, or status." Bashō is categorizing various forms of associative movement, and he takes for granted that linking of this sort is the way to move through a poem.

It is for a feeling of surprise and only retrospectively obvious connection, especially in the last line of the poem, that haiku are beloved by so many. Here is one of Ecuadorean poet Jorge Carrera Andrade's translations of the Japanese poet Yaha, translated further into English by Joshua Beckman and Alejandro de Acosta (not in strict syllabic form):

Imprisoned beneath the leaf
an anemone watches
the world's sadness pass.

No matter how many times I get to the end of that poem, I always have the same thought: I was not expecting that. Here is Bashō:

The cicada.
Nothing in its song reveals
that tomorrow it must die.

And Sora:

The coastal wind
disorders above the sea
the seagulls' wise drawings.

These haiku operate within themselves in a particularly illustrative associative manner, especially from the second to the third lines. I think what draws so many contemporary readers to haiku is not merely their simplicity or emotive calmness, but the pleasure of the associative leaps in them.

The poet Robert Bly finds this associative movement throughout poetic history, in many different forms. His book *Leaping Po-*

etry (1972) is part anthology of poetry, part critical work, and part sweetly hilarious artifact of the early 1970s (there are plenty of mentions in the book of dragons, the Great Mother, and "sexual energy"). In the book, Bly describes ancient, intuitive expressions of leaping in poetry, for example, in a poem by Pablo Neruda:

> *In "Nothing but Death," Neruda leaps from death to the*
> *whiteness of flour, then to notary publics, and he continues to*
> *make leap after leap. We often feel elation reading Neruda*
> *because he follows some arc of association which corresponds*
> *to the inner life of the objects; so that anyone sensitive to the*
> *inner life of objects can ride with him.*

Bly focuses on the leap from image to image. When looking at poetry more generally, we can see that his "arc of association which corresponds to the inner life of the objects" is a subset of a general principle of associative movement. Leaping or association in a poem is just as likely to be formal: rhyme, metaphor, quick unexpected movements in a narrative, the juxtaposition of images, and contradiction are all forms of association.

This associative movement can move among concepts, sounds (rhyme), images, or objects. As poet Tracy K. Smith wrote in the *New York Times Book Review*:

> *In a poem, association often gets you from one place to*
> *another, an image that triggers a radical shift in context*
> *or tone. And it is association that governs our experience of*
> *navigating the Web. Think of the huge leaps we take, the*
> *strange paths we wander by simply following a string of*
> *links. Everything that happens in a poem is governed by some*
> *kind of compression, but I suspect that narrative in poems is*
> *at once bigger and stranger, and more tightly compressed,*

than it was a generation ago. Then I remember "The Waste
Land," and I begin to feel that the Internet has simply
succeeded in reinvigorating a set of ambitions and capacities
that have been available to poets for a very long time.

Smith reminds us of how poems place, in close proximity,
ideas, events, moments, images that we would not ordinarily put
together. Association "gets you from one place to another," in
"leaps we take, the strange paths we wander." This is the true nar-
rative of poems, a narration of the movement of the mind.

The poet Jane Hirshfield uses the metaphor of a window to
describe this movement:

A "window," whether carpentered from the conceptual,
imagistic, or linguistic, offers a different kind of plunging.
In the swerve into some new possibility of mind, a poem with
a window stops to look elsewhere, drawing on something
outside its self-constructed domain and walls. A window can
be held by a change of sense realms or a switch of rhetorical
strategy, can be framed in a turn of grammar or ethical
stance, can be sawn open by an overt statement or slipped in
almost unseen. Whether large or small, what I am calling
a window is recognized primarily by the experience of
expansion it brings: the poem's nature is changed because its
scope has become larger.

The poetic movement of the mind in poetry has gone by many
names from the beginning of the history of literature. "Associative
movement," while to me disappointingly a bit clinical sounding,
seems to me to accurately reflect a well-known characteristic of
language: the essentially arbitrary, highly variable, yet somehow

functional relationship between words and what they attempt to stand in for. It also leaves room for a wide range of poetic practice.

AMERICAN POETS HAVE BORROWED FROM THE WIDEST POSSIBLE array of associative approaches. Some are wild heirs to the Symbolists and Surrealists. Others move their poems in calmer leaps. If to understand poetry is to allow one's mind to move with the mind of the poem, to understand contemporary American poetry in particular is to be willing to experience a great variety of associative movement and leaping.

Robert Hass's poem "Meditation at Lagunitas" appeared in his second book, *Praise*, published in 1979. Like all great poems that change our ideas about what can be done in poetry, this one has become (for better and for worse) an exemplar of a "type" of contemporary poem. It's smart and intellectual, while also full of feeling. It moves and shifts comfortably among different modes: philosophizing, psychological commentary, thoughts about the nature of language, anecdotes, natural observations, and so on.

Meditation at Lagunitas

All the new thinking is about loss.
In this it resembles all the old thinking.
The idea, for example, that each particular erases
the luminous clarity of a general idea. That the clown-
faced woodpecker probing the dead sculpted trunk
of that black birth is, by his presence,
some tragic falling off from a first world
of undivided light. Or the other notion that,
because there is in this world no one thing
to which the bramble of *blackberry* corresponds,
a word is elegy to what it signifies.

We talked about it late last night and in the voice
of my friend, there was a thin wire of grief, a tone
almost querulous. After a while I understood that,
talking this way, everything dissolves: *justice,*
pine, hair, woman, you and *I.* There was a woman
I made love to and I remember how, holding
her small shoulders in my hands sometimes,
I felt a violent wonder at her presence
like a thirst for salt, for my childhood river
with its island willows, silly music from the pleasure boat,
muddy places where we caught the little orange-silver fish
called *pumpkinseed.* It hardly had to do with her.
Longing, we say, because desire is full
of endless distances. I must have been the same to her.
But I remember so much, the way her hands dismantled
    bread,
the thing her father said to her that hurt her, what
she dreamed. There are moments when the body is as
    numinous
as words, days that are the good flesh continuing.
Such tenderness, those afternoons and evenings,
saying *blackberry, blackberry, blackberry.*

Beginning practitioners in meditation are often counseled not
to berate themselves for distracted thinking. As Pema Chödrön
writes in "The Monkey Mind," a chapter in her book *How to Medi-*
tate, "It's as natural for the mind to think as it is for the body to
breathe, or for the heart to pump blood through the veins. The mo-
tivation behind meditation is not to get rid of thoughts, but to train
the mind to reclaim its natural capacity to stay present." Especially
for beginners, and possibly especially Western ones, meditation

is mostly the practice of being attentive to one's own distracted, drifting mind, by doing something simple like, as Chödrön suggests, placing one's mind on one's breath. The practice of meditation is not merely about banishing all thoughts and just somehow being "empty." Nor does it have to be a stern self-training in strict concentration.

The title of the poem, "Meditation at Lagunitas," could refer literally to the practice of meditation, or a meditation in the more general sense; that is, an extended contemplation. Maybe the title is positing that both are the same. Here this meditative thinking takes place in Lagunitas, a small, not particularly notable town in Northern California. The word "at" in the title is a little different from what we might expect. Why not "in"? "Meditation *in* Lagunitas" would be a more normal and expected phrase, and would give us more of a feeling of the town as a place one can visit, or live in. The word "at" gives a slight air of comic solemnity to the proceedings. One could easily imagine a meditation "at" the Colosseum in Rome, or the Taj Mahal, or Mt. Everest. But Lagunitas? It is as if the poem is, with gentle irony, asserting that Lagunitas is an important place, which of course it is not—at least not yet. Perhaps it is the meditation, the poem itself, that makes the place important. What is not important becomes so through attention, particularly the attention of poetry. The events of the poem, as commonplace as they might turn out to be, as well as the thinking about those events, are in fact important enough to make the place a landmark.

Oddly, this is in fact what has happened. When this poem was first published, hardly anyone would have known about this little town in Northern California. By now among poets it's famous, not just for the poem, but also on account of a deservedly well-known eponymous brewing company. When we were younger poets my friends and I used to drink their delicious bitter beer, Lagunitas IPA, with only slightly ironic sacramental devotion; and we were proud we knew, because of the poem, how to properly pronounce it: lah-goo-NEE-tas.

"All the new thinking is about loss. / In this it resembles all the old thinking." These are arguably the most famous lines of American poetry written in the past fifty or so years. The assertion that all our "new thinking" is not new at all is, at the same time, both comforting (things aren't worse now than they have always been) and upsetting (loss is always at the center of everything). The poem moves by enacting a sort of distracted, dreamy attention, from thinking about a general idea, to specific observations about nature (the woodpecker), to language theory. These ideas "rhyme" in the sense that they have latent connections that we would not ordinarily perceive, but which are brought out by the poem. To bring out these connections, these conceptual rhymes, is one of the main purposes of the poem.

According to the poem, words are, inevitably, approximations: "there is in this world no one thing / to which the bramble of *blackberry* corresponds." And "talking this way, everything dissolves." There is an insufficiency to the way language encounters reality, a failure even, one that resembles a death. This failure occurs whenever we use the imperfect instrument of language. This might remind some of us of the many literary theorists and theories that, in various ways, assert the ultimately subjective nature of perception and how it is bound up in language.

The shift from this philosophizing to personal anecdote, as the speaker turns to talking about the friend talking about language, and then the former lover, is accomplished with grace and confidence. The poetry is in this shifting, the movement from one idea to another that is both unexpected yet also retrospectively logical.

That associative movement is what Bly calls, in *Leaping Poetry,* "a form of content." The way the mind is moving—associatively—is what the poem is "about." It could be said its "how" (form) is its "what" (content). By moving associatively, from subject to subject, the poem is asserting something about the fundamental nature of the world, and about the relations among things, relations we might not consciously perceive in our everyday lives. To create a place where our minds can experience this movement is, as much as any ideas that are expressed, the purpose of the poem.

It matters greatly, of course, that what is being said in the poem is attentive, thoughtful, surprising, and, at least for many readers, seemingly true. There is a kind of honesty and directness both in *what* is being said, as well as in *how*: the tone of the poem is that of a very smart, kind friend. There is poetry in the way the language of this poem reaches out to capture big ideas, in ways that are impossible to paraphrase or restate: "each particular erases / the luminous clarity of a general idea," "a word is elegy to what it signifies," "a thin wire of grief, a tone / almost querulous," "the way her hands dismantled bread," and of course the famous last line, the repetition of the word used earlier in the poem as an example of the insufficiency of language: *blackberry, blackberry, blackberry.* To come upon the end of the poem is, each time, to encounter a pure instance of the noble, essential, and glorious high-wire failure that seems only possible in poetry: making meaning by failing to fully make meaning, by graciously, despairingly, beautifully, capitulating to the ultimate unsayability and ultimate unknowability of it all.

This poetry—the language stretching out to almost grasp what feels like an unstated truth, in ways one cannot paraphrase without doing reductive violence to the thinking—is also a kind of association, a leap in language across the void between what we think every day and what we sense, in a deeper way, to be true.

ASSOCIATION IN POETRY CAUSES US TO SEE AND UNDERSTAND IN vital ways that would otherwise not be available. This is true for smaller, ordinary experience in life, but also for the biggest societal issues that confront us. In Terrance Hayes's poem "The Avocado," the narrator is listening to a speech about abolitionists and slavery race relations at a luncheon, growing ever hungrier as he looks at "black tortillas on a red plate beside a big green bowl / of guacamole made from the whipped, battered remains / of several harmless former avocados." The elements of the speech start combining comically with more mundane physical desires:

> . . . I'm thinking
> of the money-colored flesh of the avocado, high in
>   monosaturates;
> its oil content is second only to olives. I am looking
> at Yoyo's caterpillar locks dangle over her ear. I dare you
> to find a lovelier black woman from Cincinnati, where the
>   North
> touches the South . . . .

Here is the daydreaming tendency, central to so much poetic activity, brought out into the open. It is tactile and erotic, and does not respect categories of proper thought behavior.

The speech-giver mentions Harriet Tubman. Addled by hunger, the poet wanders ever more distracted, following whatever associations emerge:

> "Demand number twenty-one; a Harriet Tubman statue on
>   the mall!"
> Brother man is weeping now and walking wet tissue to the
>   trash can

and saying, "Harriet Tubman was a walking shadow," or,
    "Harriet Tubman
walked in shadows," or, "To many, Harriet Tubman was a
    shadow
to walk in," and the meaning is pureed flesh with lime juice,
minced garlic, and chili powder; it is salt, and the pepper
Harriet Tubman tossed over her shoulder to trouble the
    bloodhounds.
Many isolated avocado trees fail to fruit from lack of
    pollination.
"Godddamn, ain't you hungry?" I whisper to Yoyo, and she
    puts a finger
to my lips to distract me.

Even remembering an iconic, desperate, and mortal moment—
Tubman throwing pepper over her shoulder to "trouble the blood-
hounds" on her trail—he can't help but think about food and
sex and identify, mournfully and ridiculously, with the "isolated
avocado trees" that don't get to pollinate. The poem ends with
a sharp veer into seriousness, with a thought about what it re-
ally might have been like for Tubman, when, chillingly, she had
to terrify her own charges into silence in order to avoid being
caught:

    . . . . "Hush now," Harriet Tubman probably said
near dawn, pointing a finger black enough to be her pistol
    barrel
toward the future or pointing a pistol barrel black enough
to be her finger at the mouth of some starved, stammering
    slave
and then lifting her head to listen for something no one but
    her could hear.

Something vital is being said about the connections among race, sex, hunger, violence. The speaker himself cannot quite hear, or fully understand, the meaning of the story of Harriet Tubman. Does she walk in shadow? Is she a shadow? A shadow to walk in? The poem is a system of associative meaning true to the immense complexity of the situation.

LIKE RACE, ECONOMIC ANXIETY IS A CONSTANT SUBJECT OF writing, discussion, thinking. We might think everything that could possibly be said about it has already been said, and yet, there is still always something missing.

One of the best books to emerge from, and reflect, our anxious new awareness of economic fragility is Victoria Chang's 2013 collection of poetry *The Boss*. These poems throw themselves again and again into anxieties about power, work and the economy, and family (the father, slowly slipping into dementia, is a central figure in the book, as is the narrator herself as a mother). The book associates through these various elemental and familiar figures, connecting them in surprising ways.

There are little moments of narration and situation in the book, ones that would be recognizable to many readers. The voice moves through the poems with total liberation, leaping from one life area (work) to the next (family) to the next (illness) and back again. In the beginning of the book, the boss is the one we know, from our various jobs:

> I once was a child am a child am someone's child
>   not my mother's not my father's the boss
> gave us special treatment treatment for something
>   special a lollipop or a sticker glitter from the
>
> toy box the better we did the better the plastic prize made
>   in China . . .

The comparison of the workplace society to a family gives the word "boss" an immediate complexity. It turns "boss" into a field of associations. The word "treatment" is immediately defamiliarized: "special treatment," in a job context, becomes associated with another meaning, the medical one. The "us" in the poem, the workplace children, become infantilized, getting "something / special a lollipop or a sticker" as they would after a doctor's visit.

Over the course of the book the word "boss" is returned to, again and again. It becomes more resonant, polysemous, symbolic, as do the other elements of work, family, the city, and other things that surround us. The overall effect of reading the book is to feel as if one is falling into a dream where everything that is familiar is charged with painful significance, a realization of the truth of so many relations habit numbs us to.

The associative intertwining of job, family, childhood, and economic threat continues:

> . . . one year everyone got a spinning top
> one year everyone got a tap on their shoulders
>   one year everyone was fired everyone
>
> fired but me one year we all lost our words one year
>   my father lost his words to a stroke
> a stroke of bad luck stuck his words
>   used to be so worldly his words fired
>
> him let him go without notice can they do that
>   can she do that yes she can in this land she can

The lack of punctuation in the poem adds to the speed of association. Only through this type of thinking can we begin to *feel* these lightning-fast, quicksilver connections. Reading the poem, I feel they are essential for understanding our situation.

DESPITE THE INTIMATE CONNECTION OF ASSOCIATIVE MOVEment to poetic activity, it is not true that the more wildly associative the thinking, the better the poem. Just try reading more than a few lines of André Breton and Philippe Soupault's breakthrough experiments in automatic writing, in *The Magnetic Fields*: what is at first marvelous and revolutionary very soon can feel repetitive.

There is, of course, marvelous energy even to the pure automatic writing of early Surrealism. However, the truly great poems of the movement were written later, once that energy was assimilated and integrated. These poems have the feeling of not merely inventing something clever or superficially exciting, but coming upon a deeper truth. They seem to discover something essential about human life.

In his masterful introduction to *The Selected Writings of Guillaume Apollinaire*, translator, critic, and literary historian Roger Shattuck elegantly, and with great lucidity, considers the relationship between the boldness or intensity of association and the presence of poetry:

> *I spoke at the start of a criterion applicable to all art: that it should present both clarity and mystery. These terms and the evaluations they permit can now be elucidated. The clarity of a literary work of art lies in its reference to experiences already familiar and available to the reader, which allow him to orient himself within this territory called art. The mystery points toward experience not yet known, to an extension of the consciousness.*

Earlier I quoted Mahmoud Darwish, when he wrote: "Extreme clarity is a mystery." For Shattuck, the elements of a poem—the actual stuff in it, like bosses and avocados, coffins and grass—are the "clarity." They are the things that connect us as readers with the poem. The mystery of the poem is the way those things are turned toward "experience not yet known, to an extension of the consciousness," into the mysteries and contradictions that are always there in our lives.

This is why association can be most powerful for a reader when experienced as part of, and emerging naturally from, a more familiar language structure. James Tate is a poet whose later work has approached the horizon of prose. The poems in his last several books have plot, characters, and a conversational speech that is aggressively distant from what we might usually think of as poetic (compressed or beautiful or imagistic or sonically resonant language). Yet in these casual, prose-like poems there is so often something deeply poetic. As in the prose poem, the poetry comes as the shock of the associative consciousness rises suddenly out of the mundane. "Rapture," from his 2001 volume *Memoir of the Hawk*, seems at first to be about a sort of countrified charmer who makes up a story for one of the oldest of purposes.

> "If you sit here a long time and are real
> quiet, you might just get to see one of those
> blue antelope," I said to Cora. "I'd do any-
> thing to see a blue antelope," she said. "I'd
> take off all my clothes and lie completely still
> in the grass all day." "That's a good idea,"
> I said, "taking off the clothes, I mean, it's
> more natural." I'd met Cora in the library the
> night before and had told her about the blue

antelope, so we'd made a date to try and see
them. We lay naked next to one another for hours.
It was a beautiful, sunny day with a breeze that
tickled. Finally, Cora whispered into my ear,
"My God, I see them. They're so delicate, so
graceful. They're like angels, cornflower
angels." I looked at Cora. She was disappearing.
She was becoming one of them.

Out of ordinary desire comes a magical transformation, a liberation. By means of the poem the ancient mythic world of metamorphosis, where women were constantly being turned into creatures and trees in order to escape the sexual desire and predation of the gods, permeates ours.

A POEM MOVES THROUGH CONTRADICTION, CONNECTING PREVIously unlike elements so we understand in new ways. Sometimes, in doing so, a poem lands on what can feel like a great truth. So many of us come to poetry for those succinct, distilled moments. They feel true and right, just as when an unexpected, perfect metaphor clicks into place.

One of the great pleasures of reading poetry can be that encounter with aphorism: that simple, concise formulation of a thought that feels original, memorable, and somehow as if it is perfectly articulating a thought we often have but have never really been able to put into words.

A line of poetry isolated from a poem (like on a greeting card, or on Twitter) can often sound overly silly, or portentous, or obvious, when within the context of the poem it feels exactly right and resonant. This is because its aphoristic quality, its feeling of truth and rightness, depends not merely on what it is saying, but on how it appears in the poem. In this way, the truths of poetry are intimately related to associative movement.

The poems that most persist in the popular imagination very often have aphoristic endings. Auden's "Funeral Blues" memorably ends, "Pour away the ocean and sweep up the wood; / For nothing now can ever come to any good."

Even poets who usually steer away from this type of poetic behavior often are best known for certain aphoristic exceptions. In James Tate's great early poem "The Lost Pilot," the narrator addresses his father, a World War II pilot who died before the narrator was born. The narrator of the poem believes he sees his dead father "once every year of my life, / spin across the wilds of the sky / like a tiny, African god." At those moments

> I feel dead. I feel as if I were
> the residue of a stranger's life,
> that I should pursue you.
>
> My head cocked toward the sky,
> I cannot get off the ground,
> and, you, passing over again,
>
> fast, perfect, and unwilling
> to tell me that you are doing
> well, or that it was mistake
>
> that placed you in that world,
> and me in this; or that misfortune
> placed these worlds in us.

In general, aphorism at the end of the poem usually feels epiphanic, like a culmination, as if we have at last arrived at some wisdom. To end a poem aphoristically is a delicate matter: at times, the power of the ending aphorism can feel like the journey of the poem is subordinated to this final message, which is what the poem is really "about." This can give everything that came before it the feeling of an unnecessary preamble.

Some poets play with this expectation, by springing an aphoristic statement on us without much warning. Frank O'Hara's poem "The Day Lady Died" appeared in his 1954 collection *Lunch Poems*, a brilliant and pleasurable and essential book of twentieth-century American literature. The poem moves through a daytime space of distracted thinking. The speaker in the poem famously and charmingly perambulates Manhattan, doing errands such as going to the bank, where "Miss Stillwagon (first name Linda I once heard) / doesn't even look up my balance for once in her life," buying cigarettes, and liquor and books as presents, until he sees the cover of a *New York Post* with the news of the death of Billie Holiday, at which point his mind goes to a memory of being in the audience once when she sang:

> and I am sweating a lot by now and thinking of
> leaning on the john door in the 5 SPOT
> while she whispered a song along the keyboard
> to Mal Waldron and everyone and I stopped breathing

The shock both of discovering the death, and of the fact of an untimely death itself, is exactly enacted in the form of the poem, as that memory comes out of the mundanity of life, memories of a day that would only be remembered and memorialized because of the great event of the death of the singer.

At other times, an aphoristic ending can feel like an even more surprising leap. The first thirteen and a half lines of Rilke's sonnet "Archaic Torso of Apollo" meditate on this headless object, a fragment of a classical sculpture. The poem asserts that there is a hidden power to the sculpture, a "brilliance from inside, / like a lamp," one we cannot see but which must be there, because only such a hidden power could explain the effect of this torso upon its viewers. It is only in the second half of the very last line that the poem veers out into an unpredictable insight that feels retrospectively exact. Here is the end of Stephen Mitchell's translation of the poem:

> Otherwise this stone would seem defaced
> beneath the translucent cascade of the shoulders
> and would not glisten like a wild beast's fur:

> would not, from all the borders of itself,
> burst like a star: for here there is no place
> that does not see you. You must change your life.

In contemporary poetry there is an ongoing, necessary reaction against forced aphorism, too much fake wisdom. As Keats wrote in a letter, "We hate poetry that has a palpable design upon us—and if we do not agree, seems to put its hand in its breeches pocket. Poetry should be great & unobtrusive, a thing which enters into one's soul, and does not startle it or amaze it with itself but with its subject." A poem that seems full of too much knowledge, too much pleasure in its own knowingness, can be as annoying as a person with those same qualities. The poem can start to feel like some folksy bore, or a pedantic dinner guest. Sometimes, awfully, the tone is unmistakably professorial.

Poets are well aware of this pitfall. The end of mid-twentieth-century American poet James Wright's "Lying in a Hammock at William Duffy's Farm in Pine Island, Minnesota" seems to me to be deeply ironic, and pokes a little fun at Rilke's well-known ending of "Archaic Torso of Apollo," while also taking it into a different emotional realm, from idealistic Germanic awed self-realization to an American postwar sardonic depressiveness:

> To my right,
> In a field of sunlight between two pines,
> The droppings of last year's horses
> Blaze up into golden stones.
> I lean back, as the evening darkens and comes on.
> A chicken hawk floats over, looking for home.
> I have wasted my life.

"The droppings of last year's horses" are, of course, old horse-shit, which is one way of thinking about one's own poetry, and how one might have wasted his life writing it.

A poem that exaggerates and satirizes, but also enacts the full power of aphorism, is Alice Notley's marvelous long poem "The Prophet." The speaker in the poem is like some kind of contemporary Polonius, were he to have been reincarnated into the body of a brilliant young artist and mother of modest means. By the end, the poem has attained an intense momentum. Thinking and daily life are intertwined to achieve a state of wisdom, and the reader feels the assertion of this state of wisdom, as well as the meaning of what is being said, with equal force, in its final lines:

> . . . . All of us know each other. Please
> Take it easy & take care of yourself. Do not die in a
>   monument, like
> Cleopatra, unless like for Cleopatra it's the only place left to
>   go. Be a

Noble girl, whether or not you die in a monument, whatever
    your sex. Do not generally
Go about giving advice. That which is everybody's business
    is nobody's
Business. Let thyself become undeceived through the beauty
    & strangeness of
The physical world. It is almost possible to believe that if you
    look at it really see it be it for yourself
You will be free. They say it will be cloudy tomorrow but
    they
Are often wrong. There's a lot to say about two & one. Your
    life
Is not small or mean, it is beautiful & big, full of planets
    clouds skies and
Also your tiniest things of you. One is you & all this & two &
    yet. You must never
Stop making jokes. You are not great you are life.

10

ALIEN NAMES

WHEN YOU LOOK FOR IT, METAPHOR IS EVERYWHERE IN LAN-guage. The literary critic I. A. Richards wrote, "Metaphor is the omnipresent principle of language . . . We cannot get through three sentences of ordinary fluid discourse without it." Robert Frost fa-mously pointed to the pervasive presence of metaphor not just as a feature of language, but as a means of understanding the world: ". . . unless you are at home in the metaphor, unless you have had your proper poetical education in the metaphor, you are not safe anywhere. . . . You are not safe in science; you are not safe in his-tory."

Language is by its nature inherently metaphorical. Each word conceptually replaces something else: a thing, an idea, a phenom-enon, and so on. Therefore, because poetry is so interested in re-activating the material of language, in order to see what is possible when functionality is subordinated to exploration and play, poetry is full of metaphor. Metaphorical thinking is also pervasive in poetry because it is a potent and particularly electric version of the associative movement characteristic of all poetry.

A metaphor starts out as a connection our minds might never have made. But through reading the poem, we experience that connection as it happens in the mind of the poet. And so, by reading and experiencing that connection, it becomes the way we think as well. In poetry, metaphors are not merely decorative, that is, placed in the text to make it more interesting or lively or appealing. Their mechanisms are laid bare, so we can see and feel the transformation of what has become too familiar. New connections are made before our eyes, so we can feel enlivened, disturbed, renewed.

The fundamental mechanisms that make a metaphor—unexpected association, and an activation of the latent potential energy of words, along with a reminder of their dangerous and exciting provisionality—are central to poetic activity. And because poets can get very interested in the making of metaphors for their own sakes, without being beholden to any other overarching task, metaphors can have an intensity and strangeness and power in poetry that you do not feel anywhere else.

Making metaphors is a particular way of seriously playing with language. To make (or perhaps better to say, to discover) a good metaphor requires an intense focus on the meanings of words, as well as an instinctive freedom in combining them. In my own experience, the sense that there is a possibility in connecting two words that do not usually go together comes first as a mostly inchoate possibility, a desire to experiment, to start putting things together until they fit.

Often I have intuitively placed two words near each other, and then only later realized that there are latent connections and refractions of meaning of which I was not remotely aware in a conscious sense. This is both unnerving and thrilling, but I've learned to trust it, telling myself again and again not only to have faith in my decades dedicated to getting to know the material of language, but also that the complex machine of language and its collective wisdom is far more intelligent than my little consciousness could ever be. When I am at my best as a poet, I feel not like I am using language to write, but the other way around.

Aristotle wrote, "Metaphor consists of giving the thing a name that belongs to something else." Or, in another translation, "Metaphor is the application of an alien name by transference." I still think there is no better definition. Aristotle identifies the *process* (of giving, or application) as central to metaphor. Metaphor is not the original thing being compared, or what it is being compared to, but the *interaction* between the two of them. It is not merely a comparison of one thing to another, but the creation of a new, third resonance, a field of meaning.

The key word in Aristotle's definition of metaphor as "the application of an alien name by transference" is "alien." The word in Greek is "*aliotros*," often translated as "other," but I like the slightly more exotic and equally accurate "alien," because it carries with it the implication of something that comes from far away, maybe even another planet. This is what a great metaphor can feel like. There is an aura of surprise to a great metaphor, as well as an uncanny familiarity. It reminds me of when E.T. lands on earth and winds up in the little boy's closet. At first it seems impossible, but in the end the alien belongs to the boy, and vice versa.

After the fact, metaphors can seem natural and even inevitable. But for the poet in process, metaphor-making proceeds through trial and error. It might work something like this: A poet can take one word—maybe an abstraction, like love or fear or happiness, or an object, something concrete, like a flower or mountain or book—that feels for some reason full of potential energy, unexpressed meaning. The poet then gives herself the space and time and, most important, the freedom from any doctrine to try to allow her mind to leap, for no discernible reason, to another word. Then she searches for a way to connect the two. Quite often it doesn't work—there is nothing there. Maybe she tries again, maybe many more times. Sometimes one element will change, or both. Eventually something clicks, an electrical connection is made, a way is found to connect the two things, and the poem begins.

"REALITY IS A CLICHÉ FROM WHICH WE ESCAPE BY METAPHOR," Stevens wrote. I go to Stevens in my lowest moments, when I feel most separate from poetry, as if my imagination has been crushed or drained by the demands of life. In his poems, even ones I have read many times, I continually find new experiences, phrases and lines that resonate mysteriously, and seem to light up some part of my brain that has been darkened by the mundane.

Reading Stevens's poems, I feel immediately affected, interested, excited, and moved. I feel carried by them into a different space. I like having this experience not only because it is so strong, but also because I can't exactly say *why*. Even though I can almost always describe what is happening in the poems, and can point to many memorable objects—a jar in Tennessee, coffee and oranges and a cockatoo wandering on a rug, a blackbird, an old sailor dreaming of a tiger, a rabbit, a snowman, a blue guitar—I can't say exactly what the poems are *about*.

Stevens's first book, *Harmonium*, was published in 1923. A harmonium is a sort of organ you power by pumping with your hand or foot, and simultaneously play like a piano. The harmonium is a premodern, domestic instrument, self-powered by the player. If the whole book is, as Stevens implies by the title, a harmonium, the poems in the book might be thought of as little tunes, to be played as they are read. And who is the player? The reader, I think. Though these poem/tunes were written by someone else, in order for them to exist, I must play them with the air through my lungs, by speaking. To make this music we don't need electricity, or an orchestra, just the harmonium/book and the simple act of playing/reading.

This short poem from *Harmonium* is an argument for the necessity of metaphor:

Gubbinal

That strange flower, the sun,
Is just what you say.
Have it your way.

The world is ugly,
And the people are sad.

That tuft of jungle feathers,
That animal eye,
Is just what you say.

That savage of fire,
That seed,
Have it your way.

The world is ugly,
And the people are sad.

This is the first poem by Stevens that I remember reading. I immediately loved the extreme simplicity of its language, and its grouchily argumentative tone. The dictionary tells me a "gubbin" is a kind of "ironstone," a word I then also had to look up in order to discover it is in fact exactly what it sounds like, a stone with a lot of iron in it. Iron is the most common element on earth, and is therefore the opposite of precious or remarkable. A "gubbins," it turns out, is a stupid person.

The poem seems to me to be a sarcastic rejoinder to the kind of dullard who insists only on what is most practical and real, someone anti-metaphorical. For such a person, the sun is not a "strange flower," it is merely the sun, though the poet does manage through negation to sneak in a little bit of metaphorical transformation, as if to say, "Far be it from me to mention how amazing it would be if you allowed yourself to dream a little."

But other than that one instance, all other objects—jungle feathers, animal eye, savage of fire, seed—which *could* be transformed, in the imagination, in poems, here, in this poem of exasperated capitulation, are not. They remain inert, stagnant, unactivated, and unimagined. Without the transformative associative imagination activated and enacted in poems, the poem says, all those things will be "just what you say" and remain merely what they are and nothing more, so the world will continue to be merely ugly, and the people sad.

IN A LATER POEM WHICH APPEARED IN HIS 1947 VOLUME *Transport to Summer*, Stevens talks explicitly about metaphor:

The Motive for Metaphor

You like it under the trees in autumn,
Because everything is half dead.
The wind moves like a cripple among the leaves
And repeats words without meaning.

In the same way, you were happy in spring,
With the half colors of quarter-things,
The slightly brighter sky, the melting clouds,
The single bird, the obscure moon—

The obscure moon lighting an obscure world
Of things that would never be quite expressed,
Where you yourself were not quite yourself,
And did not want nor have to be,

Desiring the exhilarations of changes:
The motive for metaphor, shrinking from
The weight of primary noon,
The A B C of being,

The ruddy temper, the hammer
Of red and blue, the hard sound—
Steel against intimation—the sharp flash,
The vital, arrogant, fatal, dominant X.

The poem addresses an unnamed "you," who contradictorily likes both "half dead" autumn and "in the same way," also, the more alive, uncanny spring. After the two short, direct sentences that describe the "half dead" autumn, the rest of the poem is one long, complex sentence, which has the appearance of logic, but also a kind of elusiveness and resistance to paraphrase.

Besides being a cause or a goal, a "motive" is also another word for a musical or literary "motif," a central or guiding theme. Each time I read this poem I have the strong impression that the "motive" of the poem is to conjure that particular, elusive way it feels when everything in the world is starting to seem in the midst of a process of magical transformation, metaphorical:

The obscure moon lighting an obscure world
Of things that would never be quite expressed,
Where you yourself were not quite yourself,
And did not want nor have to be

The diffuse, obscure, reflected moonglow lights up whatever it touches in a ghostly uncanny manner, making even the most mundane object or person special and mythic, and making it possible to feel the presence of things ordinarily hidden, "things that would never be quite expressed," and even to feel the thrilling possibility of being a different person.

This moonlit obscurity allows us to see what has become too familiar in a dimmer, more mysterious light. In a true poem, what is "obscure" is not hidden away from us. Obscurity is a kind of available dimness, a light in which things can most definitely be seen, recognizable and not, familiar and unfamiliar.

As Stevens writes in the next stanza, the "motive for metaphor" is "shrinking from" what feel like certainties that follow in the poem. These certainties might be essential, but they are not everything. They are "Steel against intimation"; that is, a force that opposes something indirect, only pointed toward but not there, "things that would never be quite expressed," at least not anywhere but in poetry.

Keats once sarcastically described one of his friends, Charles Dilke, as someone "who cannot feel he has a personal identity unless he has made up his Mind about everything." This personal need for hard certainty, for "Steel" to oppose the indeterminacy of intimation, seemed to Keats to be antithetical to the poetical character. I remember as a young person being very struck by this remark, because I too had always associated maturity with certainty, with knowing the answers to everything, with having a point of view that was stable and continuous.

Poetry brings into play a countervailing force, one that pushes us toward a state of mind that can feel paradoxically both ambiguous yet full of strong, obscure, yet somehow palpable feelings, ones that do not fall into the usual categories we use to name our emotions and experiences. In "The Motive for Metaphor" Stevens is simultaneously describing, defending, and enacting this state of indeterminacy and obscurity as necessary and good, a state of being where we are not quite ourselves, and do not want or have to be.

{11}

TRUE SYMBOLS

LIKE SO MANY OF US, I NEVER MUCH ENJOYED THE SORT OF LIT-
erary analysis, pervasive in school, that required us to figure out
what the text "really" means, and what the words "stood in for,"
what my teachers and textbooks called "symbolism." Of course I
obediently performed such poetry analyses, to get good grades on
my papers and tests. But it always seemed like a waste of time to me.

Once I started writing poetry myself, and saw how so many
readers immediately assumed that the words I had written "really"
meant something other than what I was saying, and that I had
somehow composed the poems in order to hide a deeper meaning,
I liked this version of poetry even less. It was frustrating and even
heartbreaking to be trying to make something for readers, and to

have their reaction be to tell me that what I had made was a deliberate obfuscation.

Too many of us have been systematically taught to read poetry as if it is full of symbols that stand in for meanings not obviously present in the text itself. The reasons for the pervasiveness of this idea are complex. Regardless of why, so often I have seen even the simplest poem, full of single-syllable words any five-year-old knows, greeted with incomprehension. And I think one big reason is the way we have been taught to think about the genre of poetry: a place where objects are no longer what they are in the world, but symbolic.

This is something many writers, not just of poetry, have felt to be a problem for a long time. In a letter responding to the question of symbolism in *The Old Man and the Sea*, Ernest Hemingway wrote: "There isn't any symbolism. The sea is the sea. The old man is an old man. The boy is a boy and the fish is a fish. The sharks are all sharks no better and no worse. All the symbolism that people say is shit. What goes beyond is what you see beyond when you know."

"All the symbolism that people say" seems to be a casual way of talking about the sort of literary analysis familiar to so many of us from school, that attaches specific meanings to the objects in the story: old man, boy, fish equal x, y, z. So many of us have written those kinds of essays. And what have we really learned? On the other hand, it seems absurd for Hemingway, or anyone, to say that there is no symbolic meaning in the book. Anyone who has read *The Old Man and the Sea* knows that the entire book feels highly charged with symbolic meaning.

But a distinction can definitely be made between the so-called symbolism that is taught in school (really, an idea that literary works are made up of codes) and symbolic meaning, or true symbolism. True symbolism depends not on some words "standing in for" some other specific words or ideas not mentioned in the text: that kind of fake symbolism is what Hemingway means when he writes, "All the symbolism that people say is shit."

The true symbolic effect of the text depends on a magical transformation, where the things themselves—sea, old man, boy, fish, sharks—somehow remain themselves and also together create a feeling of greater meaning, one that is never specified. That is the very power of Hemingway's book, what makes it on the one hand so much more than an anecdote about some people on a boat, or on the other, a heavy-handed allegory (fish stands in for noble struggle, old man stands in for aging or human frailty or whatever, boat stands in for journey of life, etc.) which just repeats to us in obvious signs something we already know.

That last sentence of Hemingway's is characteristically enigmatic, and can be read in many ways. "What goes beyond" is I think that experience we all want from literature: to have a perception, an understanding, a feeling, an intuition, that is "beyond" what we know in ordinary life. That is "what you see" when a work of art does something to you. And what I think Hemingway is saying is that a certain kind of superficial symbolism—the idea that the words in the story or poem "stand in for" an abstract concept, making them physical for the reader, an allegory—is a kind of shortcut to that feeling, one that doesn't really work.

True symbolism is the going through, by means of the ordinary, to the "beyond." I think there is a moment in one of my poems which articulates this idea as well as I can in prose:

In this poem

every word means exactly
what it means
when we use it in every day life.

So when I say I went
to the grocery store
and felt too ashamed

to ask where are the eggs
only a very small part of me means
I have returned to report

we have by our mothers
been permanently destroyed.

Eggs are eggs, as they always are, and they are also all the things that come along with the word "egg." The egg as symbol doesn't merely stand in for one single thing (like a sign does), but carries with it a field of related meanings. The symbol is both what it is, and something more. It carries with it a complexity that is totally dependent on, without being limited by, the most literal meaning of the word.

ONE OF THE GREAT PLEASURES OF READING POETRY IS TO FEEL words mean what they usually do in everyday life, and also start to move into a more charged, activated, even symbolic realm. In poetry our familiar language can start to feel resonant with significance, more alive, even noble again. The words we use in our everyday lives always carry along with them deep reservoirs of history (personal and collective) that can, through a poem, be activated.

When I started writing this book many years ago, I thought one of my main goals would be to disprove certain pervasive, incorrect ideas about symbolism in poetry. The more I thought, and read, and wrote, the more I realized that the problem was a confusion about the meaning of the word "symbol."

In everyday life, symbols can be signs that help us communicate: red octagonal sign means stop. There are symbols in mathematics, in psychology, and so on. We see symbols in politics, or on our money: they sum up big abstract concepts into a concrete figure (like dove = peace). These symbols might do more to make us *feel* we understand something abstract than to actually help us understand it.

If what we mean by "symbol" is a word or phrase that has some specific, hidden, secret meaning, then we don't really find those very often in poetry. The idea that we do is inimical to a true experience of reading it. But there is another way of understanding the symbol, and symbolic activity, in poetry, that reveals something essential about why we are inexorably drawn to writing and reading it.

The symbol in a poem does not function the way it does in everyday life. It operates the way a metaphor does, by introducing the possibility of a comparison. But unlike a metaphor, the comparison is never completed. There is only the original thing, and the very strong *feeling* that it is going to transform, as in a metaphor, but without the other, completing term. Ed Hirsch writes in his *Poetic Glossary* that "in poetry, a symbol offers a surplus of resonance." This surplus is that strong feeling of meaning, implied but ultimately left unspecified and undefined.

A metaphor: my love is a rose. That is a completed circuit. A symbol: "The rose is obsolete," as William Carlos Williams writes:

> but each petal ends in
> an edge, the double facet
> cementing the grooved
> columns of air—The edge
> cuts without cutting
> meets—nothing . . .

In this poem, the rose isn't really being compared to anything. Rather, it is a recognizable object that, by being placed in the poem, becomes charged with the *feeling* of significance. This rose is a symbol. It contains within it all the energy of the metaphor, while also leaving a vacuum in the mind of the reader, into which her own personal intuitions, memories, ideas, and associations can rush.

It turns out that all poets are symbolists, at least to some degree. Poets are interested in the possibility of words to resonate, to *mean*, more than they usually do. Somewhere, in every poem, there are words that shine forth, are activated, light up, almost as if plugged in. This is what poetry can do for language, and for us. This is why the symbol has always been a part of poetic activity. Poets have, in all cultures and at all times, stumbled upon it as a way of making poetic meaning.

In a poem, language remains itself yet is also made to feel different, even sacred, like a spell. How this happens is the mystery of each poem, and maybe its deepest meaning. Coming upon a word, having it rise up out of the preconscious, intuitive dream-state and into the poem, either to begin or somewhere along the way or even, blissfully, at the end, is the special reward of being a poet, and a reader of poetry. By being placed into the machine of a poem, language can become activated. It is both what it is and what it means, but also something greater than the ordinary.

When language in poetry becomes resonant, and charged with meaning, it achieves a symbolic status. Whatever indignities we suffer from being semiprofessional dreamers and laconic purveyors of a literary object that, unlike novels, stories, essays, songs, or almost anything else written, most people regard on a spectrum of skepticism to scorn, all poets share the knowledge of this possibility. It is what connects us as a tribe, that and the conviction that if we do it right, you will be able to feel it too.

THE ORIGINAL FRENCH SYMBOLIST POETS—BAUDELAIRE, MAL-larmé, Verlaine, Valéry, and Rimbaud—believed that the role of the poem was to bring out a usually dormant quality in language—the symbolic—in the deeper and more mysterious sense of that word. In *Poem and Symbol*, Wallace Fowlie describes French Symbolist ideas about language in poetry, in terms of the concept of "suggestion," pointing toward something that is not explicitly there in the poem, but can be felt or intuited.

For the Symbolists, describing or interpreting reality was not enough. They wanted to find and create new realities through the poem, as if the poem is a door to a different place. Or maybe a drug. The poem is designed not to be *about*, but to *do*. And the power of the poem, the way it locates new realities and changes perception, is through the symbolic reactivation of language, of the word.

In traditional Symbolism, we can see explicitly the poem as a mechanism to circumvent our ordinary ways of making meaning, of talking "about" and "describing." The poem is designed to get us to feel the presence of higher truths, a reality that is above and beyond our mundane world. Here is Fowlie's translation of Baudelaire's dictum of Symbolism, from his book *Les Fleurs du Mal*:

Correspondences

Nature is a temple where living pillars
At times allow confused words to come forth;
There man passes through forests of symbols
Which observe him with familiar eyes.

Like long echoes which in a distance are mingled
In a dark and profound unison
Vast as night is and light,
Perfumes, colors and sounds answer one another.

There are perfumes as cool as the flesh of children,
Sweet as oboes, green as prairies
— And others, corrupt, rich and triumphant,

Having the expansion of infinite things,
Like amber, musk, myrrh and incense,
Which sing of the transports of the mind and the senses.

In the first stanza, the poem merely describes this state of being. Then, after the first stanza, the poem begins to enact it. We begin to actually pass through "forests of symbols," and the poem gets stranger as it goes on. We smell perfumes that are impossible to describe except through the strange comparisons of the third stanza: cool as the flesh of children, sweet as oboes, green as prairies, and also corrupt. All these things and sensations don't sing of *meaning*: they sing of *transport*, that is, of change and a journey away from the mundane, of both the mind and the senses.

Language has emerged from our collective memory. Over thousands of years, through collective usage and trial and error, we have defined what words do and do not mean. Every time we use a word, we are, unbeknownst to us, reflecting and ratifying and perhaps slightly altering the result of all the decisions about what a word means. Our "tree" is a collective version of everyone's trees, and my tree is my version of the collective tree.

The poetic symbol operates, as all language does, collectively. Yet it resonates in the mind of a particular reader. It is why some poems last: it is possible to feel close to someone who lived thousands of years before, about whom we know very little, who wrote in a different language, and whose poems we only have, for the most part, in fragments.

> People do gossip
>
> And they say about
> Leda, that she
>
> once found an egg
> hidden under
>
> wild hyacinths
>
> *(trans. Mary Barnard)*

> they say Leda once found a hyacinth-colored egg hidden
> *(trans. Anne Carson)*

In these two versions of a fragment of a poem by Sappho, "they" tell a story about Leda, that she once found the hidden egg. It was either under hyacinths, or was hyacinth-colored. Why would people talk or gossip about this at all? To find this egg under these flowers that bloom in spring is an ordinary thing that could happen in real life, but the act also seems to resonate with unstated significance.

What eggs and hyacinths actually *are* matters greatly in creating the field of significance of the poem. Some of the associations we have with eggs are obvious: they are life containers, fragile, belonging to a mother, et cetera. Some of us also will know what hyacinths are, the way they look and smell.

The poem does not tell us what the significance is, what it all means. There is no single meaning or interpretation. The poem creates a feeling of mystery in the ordinary: to stumble upon it in the right mood can make a reader feel like the girl herself, finding the egg under the hyacinth flowers.

Because of the open-ended nature of the symbols, the poem easily lends itself to further association. Any particular reader, having personal or even private associations with eggs and flowers, is very likely to feel the poem resonate in personal ways. Those mental resonances are not "in" the poem per se, but they are a legitimate effect of it.

Matsuo Bashō (1644–1694) was one of the greatest of the Japanese haiku poets. Here is one of his best-known haiku:

> The autumn full moon:
> All night long
> I paced round the lake.

In this poem, the speaker pacing around the lake all night is in some kind of relation to the "autumn full moon." Does he feel as if the moon supports and encourages him? Reproaches him? Ignores him? It's impossible actually to say. I think it would be wrong to call this a joyful poem: pacing all night is the act of someone who is frustrated, or at least agitated.

But, more than anything, the emotional quality of the poem, its tone, depends on the mood of the reader. The meaning of the poem is generated by the relations among the elements—autumn, full moon, night, the person pacing, the lake—and by the movement of the mind through the poem. We don't know what the person is thinking about, because the poem doesn't say. So we too pace all night, around a lake, looking up at the full moon and thinking.

There are various ways haiku create a feeling of great significance and meaning out of smallness. Part of the reason haiku feel so meaningful is the very *fact* of their smallness: the contrast with the feeling of expansion as the haiku resonates. Like a symbol, it can feel as if it has a surplus of unspecified, yet highly charged, meaning. The knowledge that this has been accomplished in such a small space is exhilarating to so many readers, and intoxicating to poets. As Ecuadorean poet Jorge Carrera Andrade wrote in a 1940 essay, "Origin and Future of the Microgram," "It might seem almost impossible to enclose the great movement of the universe in such a narrow space. But through a kind of magic, the poet manages to make the infinite enter into that small cell. There, every surprise may fit."

ANOTHER MAGIC OF THE SYMBOL IS HOW IT CAN BRING A POET and a reader together across time and space. In an early poem, "Dear Reader," James Tate begins with despair at the distance between him and his reader, a despair which initially explodes in a kind of aggression, imagining the reader as dead, in a casket. The poem then settles into bleak communion:

> Dear Reader
>
> I am trying to pry open your casket
> with this burning snowflake.
>
> I'll give up my sleep for you.
> This freezing sleet keeps coming down
> and I can barely see.
>
> If this trick works we can rub our hands
> together, maybe
>
> start a little fire
> with our identification papers.
> I don't know but I keep working, working
>
> half hating you,
> half eaten by the moon.

The impossible, contradictory, burning snowflake is, itself, the symbol the poet is using to try to pry open the casket of the reader.

In "Crossing Brooklyn Ferry," Whitman acknowledges the simultaneously mundane and mysterious fact that readers of the future will hear his voice in their heads. He assures these future readers that he is with them, in their same fears and concerns:

> What is it then between us?
> What is the count of the scores or hundreds of years between
>   us?
>
> Whatever it is, it avails not—distance avails not, and place
>   avails not,
> I too lived, Brooklyn of ample hills was mine,
> I too walked the streets of Manhattan island, and bathed in the
>   waters around it,
> I too felt the curious abrupt questionings stir within me. . . .
>
> It is not upon you alone the dark patches fall,
> The dark threw its patches down upon me also,
> The best I had done seem'd to me blank and suspicious . . .

It doesn't matter, it avails not, the distances in time and place between poet and reader. Whether it is a few moments or years or longer after its completion, there is always the possibility that when a reader reads the poem, the poet and reader will at last be together, no matter how unlikely or difficult it might have been to get there. For Whitman, the "curious abrupt questionings," his feeling of questioning uncertainty, is what links him to whoever is reading the poem. He feels a kinship across time, to someone who has not yet been born, who he hopes and believes will read his poem and feel that questioning too. The "dark patches" are a great symbol that can link a reader to Whitman. Were those "dark patches" actual shadows? Of buildings? Or clouds? Or a feeling he had in himself that can only be expressed in those words? In saying them in the poem, Whitman conjures them in us too.

CHILDREN HAVE AN INTUITIVE SENSE OF THE SYMBOLIC NATURE of objects. This is why poems that get close to the consciousness of a child can feel so much more than merely nostalgic. They can bring back truths we have forgotten.

When I look back at one of the first poems I loved, "Sestina" by Elizabeth Bishop, I see that a great part of its effect on me had to do with how it creates symbolic meaning by returning to the mind of a child. A sestina is a type of formal poem in which six specific end words—in this case, "house," "grandmother," "child," "almanac," "stove," "tears"—repeat in a specific pattern. Here are the first several stanzas:

> September rain falls on the house.
> In the failing light, the old grandmother
> sits in the kitchen with the child
> beside the Little Marvel Stove,
> reading the jokes from the almanac,
> laughing and talking to hide her tears.
>
> She thinks that her equinoctial tears
> and the rain that beats on the roof of the house
> were both foretold by the almanac,
> but only known to a grandmother.
> The iron kettle sings on the stove.
> She cuts some bread and says to the child,

It's time for tea now; but the child
is watching the teakettle's small hard tears
dance like mad on the hot black stove,
the way the rain must dance on the house.
Tidying up, the old grandmother
hangs up the clever almanac

on its string. Birdlike, the almanac
hovers half open above the child,
hovers above the old grandmother
and her teacup full of dark brown tears.
She shivers and says she thinks the house
feels chilly, and puts more wood in the stove.

The poem has also always reminded me of my own childhood. I grew up in an old house, in the suburbs of Maryland. Before my family bought it, the house was owned by two unmarried sisters, who lived there together until their old age. When we moved in, the furnace and stove were strikingly old, and even after more than forty years I can see them in my mind's eye. Gradually these things were replaced, but I always felt the presence of this older, shadow version of the house, still living somehow in the new forms.

Later, when I learned more about this poem, I discovered it recalls Bishop's lonely childhood in Nova Scotia, the old house where she lived with her grandmother. For a long time I didn't know this as a specific biographical fact, but I could have intuited the outlines of it, if not the details. Most of all, though, out of all the poems about childhood, what brought me close initially to this particular poem, and why I return to it, has to do with the way these six simple repeating words gradually take on meaning and resonance as the poem goes on.

Through its repetition of these six words, the poem taps into the elemental loneliness and boredom, but also the feeling of unsaid significance, of being a child. The poem ends with the possibility of a creative life:

It was to be, says the Marvel Stove.
I know what I know, says the almanac.
With crayons the child draws a rigid house
and a winding pathway. Then the child
puts in a man with buttons like tears
and shows it proudly to the grandmother.

But secretly, while the grandmother
busies herself about the stove,
the little moons fall down like tears
from between the pages of the almanac
into the flower bed the child
has carefully placed in the front of the house.

Time to plant tears, says the almanac.
The grandmother sings to the marvelous stove
and the child draws another inscrutable house.

As the same six words repeat in different combinations at the ends of the lines, the poem takes on a momentum and logic of its own. The child perceives the almanac saying it is time to plant "tears" instead of seeds, thus conjuring a cycle of sadness and mourning inextricable with the most fundamental realities of our presence on earth. She is aware of the grandmother in her happy loneliness singing, not to another person, but to a stove. And she stands outside herself ("I is another," as Rimbaud wrote in a letter), seeing herself drawing "another inscrutable house," attempting perhaps to comfort herself, or at least trying to make sense, over and over through drawing and redrawing, of what it means to be at home.

By the time we get to the end of the poem, we feel that these six words can take on exceptional resonances, by being placed in a poem. In this way, in coming alive and being more than they are, they enact the hope of the child, to move beyond the ordinary. Each of these six talismanic objects seems both completely real and also connected to deeper, unspoken, only intuited truths.

WHEN I WAS A CHILD, MY FATHER WORKED A LOT. WHEN I WOKE up in the morning he was already gone, and he would come home late at night, and also work many weekends. He was always "at the office." This word "office," such a fixture of my childhood, is probably one reason why I have always been drawn to a poem by Robert Hayden, "Those Winter Sundays." Even though Hayden's father was, very much unlike mine, a manual laborer, and even though the young Hayden's childhood and mine could not have been more radically different (he grew up poor and African American in Detroit), the poem draws me close.

The poem begins by describing the father getting up and going to work, even on Sundays. The young speaker sleeps later, and only when "the rooms were warm" is he woken by his father, to whom he speaks ungratefully.

> Sundays too my father got up early
> and put his clothes on in the blueblack cold,
> then with cracked hands that ached
> from labor in the weekday weather made
> banked fires blaze. No one ever thanked him.

I'd wake and hear the cold splintering, breaking.
When the rooms were warm, he'd call,
and slowly I would rise and dress,
fearing the chronic angers of that house,

Speaking indifferently to him,
who had driven out the cold
and polished my good shoes as well.
What did I know, what did I know
of love's austere and lonely offices?

Those items in the poem are what they are, but also seem to resonate with greater meaning: they are symbolic of the way this father demonstrates his love and care, but in a way that cannot be adequately paraphrased. The poem takes those ordinary items and reanimates them with significance. The indifference in the mind of the child is counteracted, retrospectively, with a sense that the shoes can, like the items in a Catholic mass, become more than what they otherwise are.

This symbolic infusion of meaning culminates with the word "offices." When I was a child, I often heard that word, though more often in the singular. The very idea of the office, and the word itself, therefore became both an actual place and also symbolic. That word contained many unspoken, palpable realities. It was where my father went, and also what he did. I didn't know or understand what exactly it meant, but I knew it was significant.

For me, the feeling in the poem is similar to the indifference and taciturn hostility with which, to my great shame and eternal regret, I used to treat my father, who, when I got old enough to drive, would let me use his old car to go to school, as long as I would drop him off at the subway. The poem ends with a particular question that is also, of course, a much greater one as well:

> What did I know, what did I know
> of love's austere and lonely offices?

Through this ending, with the emotional logic of its repetition, that unexpected final word "offices" becomes endlessly reactivated for me. Nowadays "offices" is mostly used to refer to the space where work is done, but it used to mean "responsibilities," particularly ecclesiastical ones. Through Hayden's poem, the word has a dignity to it, a respect that comes from the mind of the child, who thinks of the ordinary as a holy thing. And the very unexpectedness of this word in the poem in great part is the significance of the poem itself: the way the reader comes upon the holy specialness of the word "offices" is so much like the way the child came upon that feeling too, suddenly understanding a dignity within the mundane.

A CONTEMPORARY COLLECTION THAT RESONATES WITH OLD symbolic technique, in the manner of the best haiku, while also moving symbolism into our current time, is Joshua Beckman's *The Inside of an Apple*. These short, mostly untitled poems are slightly driftier and not as concentrated as haiku, but have a similar quality of gently capturing great physical and psychological dramas in small spaces. Often in the poem there is an "I" speaking, but we don't know much about this person, other than that he lives sometimes in nature, at other times in town, and that he is (at least judging from the poems) alone most of the time.

Much of the energy in the poems comes from how ordinary objects in them are always becoming, through the act of selection itself, significant, symbolic. It's as if the poems are asserting, through an infusion of importance that is never specified, that ordinary life everywhere has potential magic, which is a kind of hope. Here, it's a shell:

> shell plucked
> from the stony shore
>   and kept around
> for this big house to enclose

>   a plaster bath
>   a room and shutter
> the windows a wind

>   my bedroom quiet
> warm and clean

>   flap flap
>   go the
>   dying
> yellow leaves

The logic of the first line of the poem is more complicated than it first seems: the purpose of keeping the shell "around" is to give the "big house" something "to enclose." This odd way of looking at an ordinary object feels interesting, as if to suggest something about a reversal in the ordinary arrangements of need and connection. Every movement in the book is thought through in this way, and the purpose of the book seems to be to conjure up in the poet himself, as well as in us, a deep attention to objects and sensations, and then to see what emerges out of such attention.

What emerges is a music that takes over the entire being of the poet, until the essence of that being—his soul—itself becomes music:

> Let my still dark soul
> be music. A made whistle
> floating out a window
> arranged.

> Some little thing
> fell and I picked it up
> and up it kept on going.

The music floats out the window. The unspecified feeling of arrangement itself, the sense that things *can* be arranged, *can* signify, is what this poem creates.

The poet picks up some unspecified "little thing," and somehow, magically, "up it kept on going." Everything the poet sees thrums with unnameable significance, and every place the poet turns his eyes to seems to be full of meaning. He looks first at the sky, then down at the ground.

> Eight dead stars
> make a sickle,
> and the earth is covered in grass.

The poem ends with a return to metaphor, and a paradoxical consolation:

Yeah, well
   my heart's a bean
      wind knocking
         windows
      and in the air
  again I hear
     thin happy music
  about being alone

In the air, the poet hears music. He is alone, but all things, ordinary and otherwise, speak to him, keep him company, because he writes poems.

12

MOST OF THE STORIES HAVE
TO DO WITH VANISHING

EARLY ON IN MY LIFE AS A POET, I HAD COME ACROSS W. S. MER-
win's poems, and fallen in love especially with his dark and often
surreal late-1960s volumes, such as *The Lice*. Those books were so
important to me, as a poet and person, but when I was in graduate
school at UMass Amherst, not many of my fellow students seemed
to share my enthusiasm. Merwin was going through a period when
he was less in fashion. Despite or perhaps because of this, we read
Merwin's *The Vixen* in a contemporary poetry course taught by
James Tate.

It was the spring of 1999, and I have, associated with this book,
a memory of sad, warm days. I loved being an MFA student, al-
though I was very unhappy all the time, mostly without realizing

it. I constantly read poetry, and wrote all sorts of poems (laboriously, on a manual typewriter I had salvaged from my grandparents' attic), all of them failures. I was lucky enough to have Tate and Dara Wier and Agha Shahid Ali as teachers. All three were calm in their behavior and unpredictable in their interests, and all three were writing with great force and power.

My fellow students were bright and nervous, and we all had the sense that something very important was starting to happen, even if we didn't know exactly what it was. At the time, we barely thought about publishing in magazines, much less publishing a book. Of course, we wanted to, but that was really for "later." Almost everything we wrote we shared with one another and then changed or threw away or reused for some other purpose. We very much thought of ourselves as experimenters, practicers, apprentices.

My paperback copy of *The Vixen* is a very light tan color, with what looks like a painting of a fox on the cover. Actually, it's a not a painting or drawing, but a blurry, impressionistic photograph by Minoru Taketazu, presumably from his book *Fox Family: Four Seasons of Animal Life*. It is described on Amazon with the following irresistible, tragic synopsis: "The life cycle of the Ezo fox, native to the northern islands of Japan, is captured in a photographic essay that follows the fox through the icy winter and birth of cubs in the spring to the family break up in the fall."

When I open the book, I see it's a first edition. I'm sure I must have bought it when it first came out in paperback, at Wootton's, a small bookstore right on the main drag in Amherst, where we went almost every day to lurk and wait to see who else would come in to hang out. On the first blank page before the title page, in pencil I see in my handwriting

Wed 23 11:30

Tue 29 2:00

Wed 30 11:30

and it takes me just a few seconds to realize these are reminders of times I was scheduled to meet my new analyst, with whom I still, all these years later, speak, on the phone now from California.

At that time, my unhappiness, which I had always just taken for granted, had recently taken on the particularly virulent, malevolent, self-destructive form of a triangular love affair. All the time I was trying to write poems, I remember being very frustrated, in a poetic sense as well as a personal one. Looking back on those early poetic efforts now, I can see, with a little tolerance and forgiveness, that I was just starting to really understand the possibilities of language as material, in the same way a painter might start at some early point to truly begin to know paint. But at the time, I was deep in the middle of many interrelated crises of confidence and couldn't see any way forward, except to thrash wildly in one aesthetic direction or another in the hope something would stick.

Some of my difficulties were inherent to the condition of being a novice. Some, however, were a result of the times. In the late 1990s, it was taken for granted, widely in poetry and especially in many of the top graduate programs in creative writing, that it was unsophisticated, retrograde, even manipulative to sully whatever was "poetic" in a poem with any kind of story or situation. Everyone knew that a poet had to relinquish the crutch of narrative to write true poetry and not merely its sad cousin, lyrical prose. To call a poem "narrative" was just a euphemism for square, unsophisticated, sappy, self-absorbed, and old-fashioned.

It was therefore a silent article of faith among the students (though not the professors) that any sort of anecdotal narration was by its nature incompatible with poetry. Of course, even a cursory study of poetry from almost any time period would quickly reveal this aesthetic position as unfounded. Yet this was an idea nestled firmly in the minds of many young poets at the time, including my friends and me. When I think back on it now, I remember that this rejection of narrative was also bound up in an idea about who had the "right" to speak. At all costs, we young poets wanted to avoid the possibility of being caught out as writers who took on, unintentionally or otherwise, oracular, superior stances in our poems that made it seem as though we thought we were better than our readers.

Surely it was good and right that we were questioning the role of the speaker in poems. American poetry had time and again fallen into what Keats called Wordsworth's "egotistical sublime," an ostensible celebration of nature, or the world, that was really about praising the poet's own superior qualities of perceptiveness. We still see this today, in those typical poems in which someone goes for a walk in the woods or to a hospital to visit a sick loved one, and sees something beautiful and terrible that reveals the supposed truth of our existence. These poems have the not-so-secret agenda of holding the sensitivity and emotional depth of the poet (and by extension the reader, who is wise and thoughtful and cultured and emotionally advanced enough to be experiencing this marvelous poem) up for collective admiration.

What we didn't realize was that this stance of the egotistical sublime, however odious, was not inherently related to the use of narrative in poetry. What we wanted was beauty that obliterated all other consideration, that lyricism, that singing that can happen only in poetry. And it was right for us to want that. But we also didn't realize how incredibly unhelpful it would inevitably be, especially as beginners in the art, to take such a rigid and unnecessary stance that narrative could not, because of its very nature, coexist with the lyric.

THE TONE OF *THE VIXEN* IS ELEGIAC, MYSTERIOUS, HISTORICAL. Centuries can go by in a few lines, and in many of the poems, a cyclical, prehistorical time can permeate the modern era. The speaker has bought an old house somewhere in rural France. He walks and meets people, some of whom seem like ghosts from a different, ancient time. Something in his life is ending ("this time / was a time of ending this time the long marriage was over / the orbits were flying apart"), and there are symbolic echoes, not too heavy-handed but definitely present, of this ending in the condition of the old house, which must be rebuilt, as well as in the reappearance of this female fox, the vixen, in real and mythic ways. On his walks, the narrator encounters various inhabitants of the rural area where he finds himself. Some of the poems are dreams, some are general meditations about the time of the narrator's life, and some take place in a much older, sometimes medieval, sometimes mythic time.

The Vixen begins with a three-page poem, "Fox Sleep." Like an overture, in its five sections the poem moves through the various times and modes of consciousness that will appear and reappear in the rest of the poems of the book. The form of "Fox Sleep" is the same as all the rest of the poems in the book: long lines that extend almost to the right margin, every other line indented, no punctuation.

Fox Sleep

On a road through the mountains with a friend many years
    ago
      I came to a curve on a slope where a clear stream
flowed down flashing across dark rocks through its own
      echoes that could neither be caught nor forgotten
it was the turning of autumn and already
      the mornings were cold with ragged clouds in the hollows
long after sunrise but the pasture sagging like a roof
      the glassy water and flickering yellow leaves
in the few poplars and knotted plum trees were held up
      in a handful of sunlight that made the slates on the silent
mill by the stream glisten white above their ruin
      and a few relics of the life before had been arranged
in front of the open mill house to wait
      pale in the daylight out on the open mountain
after whatever they had been made for was over
      the dew was drying on them and there were few who
          took that road
who might buy one of them and take it away somewhere
      to be unusual to be the only one
to become unknown a wooden bed stood there on rocks
      a cradle the color of dust a cracked oil jar iron pots
wooden wheels iron wheels stone wheels the tall box of a
          clock
      and among them a ring of white stone the size of an
embrace set into another of the same size
      an iron spike rising from the ring where the wooden
handle had fitted that turned it in its days as a hand mill

you could see if you looked closely that the top ring
that turned in the other had been carved long before in the
form
of a fox lying nose in tail seeming to be
asleep the features worn almost away where it
had gone around and around grinding grain and salt
to go into the dark and to go on and remember

This first section of the poem is essentially a description of things the speaker and his friend see on a trip together in the mountains, particularly an old mill, which has the objects that used to be inside it now "arranged . . . to wait pale in the daylight out on the open mountain / after whatever they had been made for was over"; that is, they are now antiques, for sale. It is not merely that these objects are no longer useful to their particular owners: the entire way of life that gave them a context is gone, "whatever they had been made for was over." The thought movement is, because of the lack of punctuation, fundamentally paratactic; the grammatical structure puts thoughts and events that in ordinary writing are usually organized hierarchically instead on the same plane, creating unexpected connections. As in so much contemporary poetry, the thinking is by its very nature associative, moving from one to another related, but not necessarily predictable, idea.

In other words the poem is quick, leaping, intuitive. These qualities are, however, counterbalanced by the anecdotal and narrative: "On a road through the mountains with a friend many years ago / I came to a curve on a slope . . ." This narrative grounding situates the poem firmly, which then allows the poet to step out at will and make associations and observations and digressions that are often quite strange but always believable.

It is precisely this generous willingness to establish a narrative framework that allows the poet very quickly to move into a deeper state of perception: "I came to a curve on a slope where a clear stream / flowed down flashing across dark rocks through its own / echoes that could neither be caught nor forgotten." This movement, so natural and strange, is characteristic not only of this poem but also of Merwin's poetry throughout his career. It operates like a painting by Cézanne, an artist in whom we can clearly see figuration starting in a self-conscious way to move toward abstraction, or the music of Coltrane or the Velvet Underground or Sonic Youth, who ground compositions in melody in order to be able to bring the listener along into the far regions of chaos and noise and then return.

I OFTEN SAY TO MY STUDENTS—AND IT IS STILL SO FUNNY AND strange to me to think that I am no longer a student but am a teacher myself, because in my mind, especially in relation to poetry, I will always be one—that without clarity, it is not possible to have true mystery. By clarity, I mean a sense in the reader that what is being said on the surface of the poem is not a scrim or a veil deliberately hiding some other hidden, inaccessible certainty. Clarity for me in poetry is a kind of generosity, a willingness to be together with the reader in the same place of uncertainty, striving for understanding. To give the impression that something important is happening but that the mere reader cannot, without some kind of special, esoteric knowledge, have access to it strikes me as deeply ungenerous, even cruel.

Merwin's poems have always been mysterious, generous, and clear, knowing in their unknowingness. Often this effect is achieved by means of telling a simple story. In this book, as in much of Merwin's poetry, the combination of narrative structure and associative/paratactic movement together make it possible for Merwin to do something else essential to the effect of these poems: to move quietly and confidently into an aphoristic, truth-telling mode that is somehow full of deep, personal compassion yet also disembodied. These aphoristic moments seem almost to emerge from the natural world as truths as undeniable as animals or weather.

Beneath their simple, generous surfaces, the poems are also often very complex, especially in their treatment of time. "The Furrow" begins in contemplation and ends in aphorism and there-fore seemed at the time I first read it quite unfashionable, not only in its noble and unironic willingness to explore the psychology of the narrator but also in its overt thinking about the landscape as a metaphorical way to understand a human situation.

The Furrow

Did I think it would abide as it was forever
    all that time ago the turned earth in the old garden
where I stood in spring remembering spring in another place
    that had ceased to exist and the dug roots kept giving up
their black tokens their coins and bone buttons and shoe nails
    made by hands and bits of plates as the thin clouds
of that season slipped past gray branches on which the early
    white petals were catching their light and I thought I
    knew
something of age then my own age which had conveyed me
    to there and the ages of the trees and the walls and houses
from before my coming and the age of the new seeds as I
    set each one in the ground to begin to remember

what to become and the order in which to return
    and even the other age into which I was passing
all the time while I was thinking of something different

The "it" of the first line refers to the nearest antecedent, the furrow. The speaker is asking himself if, when he first dug the furrow and planted the seeds, he thought that it, this strip of dug-up earth, would always "abide as it was forever," continue for all time to be there the way it was. Of course, part of him did not, because he was planting seeds, which he presumably thought (or at least hoped) would grow. But part of him probably did assume or think (even though his conscious mind would have been aware in a logical sense that this was not the case) that the earth would always stay this way: dug up, disrupted, in a state of change.

In addition to the basic meaning of the first line and beyond this particular situation of gardening, this question obviously has a larger, more allegorical context. It seems not merely to be the furrow but also an unspecified feeling, maybe a state of being or a time in life. It's hard to say at the beginning of the poem. The peculiar combination of specificity (the furrow) and multiple possibility (the unspoken huge feeling or idea to which the word "it" also points) is what gives the poem its immediate air of significance. A furrow is, literally, an agricultural term. But it is also, more familiarly for most people, what a forehead does when one is confused or troubled. A reader can easily imagine the narrator, who in the third line is thinking about a previous stage in his life, with a furrowed brow, trying (like the reader!) to think through something important.

The more closely I read the poem, the more I realize how complex it is, especially in its relationship to time. There are, actually, at least four different time periods in the poem. There is the current time, when the speaker is looking at the garden. There is the earlier spring, when the narrator made the furrow and planted the seeds. And there is the spring earlier than that one, the one that the narrator is remembering he remembered as he planted: "I stood in spring remembering spring in another place / that had ceased to exist." And then there is the much older time when these objects—"their black tokens their coins and bone buttons and shoe nails / made by hands and bits of plates"—first found their way into the earth the narrator is digging up. So underneath this seemingly simple poem is actually a complex layering of time and memory. Now, in the current time, looking at the garden, the narrator remembers how he thought at the time when he was planting that he knew something important about life: "I thought I knew / something of age then my own age which had conveyed me / to there and the ages of the trees and the walls and houses / from before my coming and the age of the new seeds as I / set each one in the ground."

Maybe he did know something important then. But he knows something even more important now. At that time, even though all he could see was change and disruption and the hope and efforts to start something new, a new stage in his own life was already coming to be. The poem ends with a statement that is not only particular to this narrator's life and experience but also feels aphoristic: we are always passing into new stages, while all the time we are thinking of something different. In isolation, this seems banal, but when this statement is reached at the end of the poem, it has the force of quiet revelation. Paradoxically, wonderfully, when such statements seemingly come out of nowhere—reached by associative methods and not by accretive logic—they feel all the more convincing. And this, I think, is one of the things readers truly love about poetry, this ability to hear wisdom that feels truly wise yet also disembodied, as though it comes from the world itself.

At the end of another poem from *The Vixen*, "White Morning," the speaker and some other people go out to cut branches from trees in order to "cut handles that would last." The final lines of the poem cycle through many of the modes I have mentioned above, to chilling effect:

> the crows were calling around me to white air
> I could hear their wings dripping and hear small birds with
>   lights
> breaking in their tongues the cold soaked through me I
>   was able
> after that morning to believe stories that once
>   would have been closed to me I saw a carriage go under
> the oaks there in full day and vanish I watched animals there
>   I sat with friends in the shade they have all disappeared
> most of the stories have to do with vanishing

A lot can be learned from the movement in these lines. There is the precision of natural description; a strangely accurate synesthetic way of describing birdsong that seems to come from deep attention ("small birds with lights / breaking in their tongues"); introspection ("I was able / after that morning to believe stories that once / would have been closed to me"); the temporal dislocation of seeing this carriage, maybe from a different era, that appears and disappears; the calm, precise description of huge life changes ("I sat with friends in the shade they have all disappeared"), the destabilization of which seems echoed in the absence of expected punctuation, the quickness of the line; and the final swerve into an observation that refers to the anecdote he has just told, about the carriage, the animals, the friends, but which also takes on a larger, more general significance, applicable to all of life.

Mostly though, reading them again and again, those last two lines of the poem fill me with many things: sweet, contradictory agreement that "most of the stories" in these poems, and maybe poetry in general, do in fact "have to do with vanishing"; with sadness for the fact that so many of my beloved ones from the days when I first read *The Vixen* have, like the "friends in the shade," also vanished to me now; and also with joy in remembering the possibility of that particular sudden awareness that reading and writing poems can at any time bring to me.

13

NOTHING IS THE FORCE THAT RENOVATES THE WORLD

THE FIRST, AND I THINK ONLY, POETRY READING I EVER WENT
to with my father was at a bookshop next to Washington Square
Park in Manhattan. It was afternoon, and there were two poets
reading. I remember at lunch we had eaten and drunk to our sat-
isfaction and beyond, so as soon as the first poet began, my father
almost immediately fell asleep in his chair, leaning back his head,
quietly snoring. I didn't wake him.

The second poet began. His voice was much quieter than the
first, and the whole room seemed to focus down into it. My father's
eyes opened, his head snapped a bit alarmingly forward, and he
stared at the poet the entire time while he read.

Afterward my father came up to me among the shelves and
said, I loved that, even though I didn't understand it. He repeated

that sentence over and over, confused and distressed. I didn't know what to say. A part of me wishes I had found a way just to ask him what the poems made him think of, what they brought up in his mind. I would have loved to hear it; it would have been such a different way of getting to know my father, impossible now.

In the end, though, I know it was good for this experience to remain private. It could never have been truly translated or explained. To emerge from sleep, to hear the poems and follow and join them with a gradually waking mind, to understand them and even love them in a way that comes from language, but is beyond the ability of language to describe . . . this may very well have been a nearly perfect experience to have with poetry, especially for someone inclined to be skeptical of it. Despite its ordinary resistance to poetry, my father's sleepy, drifting attention slipped easily into the associating movement of the mind of that second reader, the great Slovenian poet Tomaž Šalamun, and then continued in its own private directions.

This mutual yet separate experience with poetry my father and I had that afternoon was one of the times I felt closest to him. I knew he was getting to feel some version of what I am always searching for, in my life as a reader and writer of poetry. The power of that experience for each of us, and for us together, was inseparable from the limits to which great poetry brings us: the limits of knowledge, of language, of our own existence.

I HAVE FOUND THAT THE POEMS WHICH HAVE MEANT THE MOST to me, to which I return again and again, retain a central unsayability, a place where the drama of truly looking for something essential that can never quite be reached is expressed. Somewhere in the poem, or at its end, knowingness stops. You can feel the intelligence in the poem truly exploring, clambering along the words and down the page, and also that intelligence stopping at what cannot be known. Those moments where a limit is reached can often be the greatest, and most honest, in poetry. They can come first as a surprise, then immediately afterward feel inevitable, at least for a little while.

Once in a lecture I heard the poet Ralph Angel say, "Poetry has always existed and always will exist, because there will always be the need to say that which cannot be said." "The lyric," writes Fanny Howe in her essay "Bewilderment," "is a method of searching for something that cannot be found." Poetry, by nature, brings us up to the limit of what we can know, and in great part, this is why it exists and continues to be written.

This is why asking for a certain kind of knowledge—that way of knowing we automatically, and justifiably, expect from other texts, anything other than a poem—limits our experience with poetry. If we imagine a poem as something to be answered or solved, we will most likely find ways to do so. But I think we would be better off to think of "understanding" in a poem as an ongoing process of attention.

Simone Weil writes that attention is the purest form of generosity. A generous, open, genuinely focused attention moves us through the poem, just as it moves us through an experience, through a friendship, through anything else that means and keeps on meaning. If a poem is really good, you can't really say what it's "about," that is, what its central "message" is, any more than you can do so for a painting or a piece of music or a person or a mountain.

In response to a question after a lecture at New York University, about how to understand poetry and what it means, the poet Joshua Beckman said the following: "If you imagine the poem is a question to be answered, once you've answered the question, you move on." The quality of a great poem might very well be not only the impossibility, but the undesirability, of feeling as if it can ever be completely "understood," that the experience of reading the poem could ever be finished.

A poem is like a person. The more you know someone, the more you realize there is always something more to know and understand. A final understanding could probably only begin upon permanent separation, or death. This is why we come back to certain poems, as we do to places or people, to experience and reexperience, to see ourselves for who we truly are, and to continue to be changed.

MY FATHER AND I HAD ALWAYS HAD DIFFICULTY UNDERSTANDing each other. Naturally I loved him, and naturally too I fought with him. I was his eldest son, and there was something archetypal about our battles.

This was especially true about my choice to become a poet. During his life, we were never really able to connect around poetry. Before he died, I had already started to think about writing this book, but never got a chance to talk with him about it.

It pains me for many reasons that we were never able to find a way to talk about poetry, especially because, as it turns out, poets and lawyers have a similar relation to language. My dad was a tax lawyer. This profession is much less boring than it sounds, which is (as my father often said) very. One idea I really wish I could have run by him is that there is something unexpectedly akin in our mutual fascination with the exact meanings of words, and where the limits to those meanings reside.

Lawyers who specialize in taxation are deeply involved in the intricate problems of contracts and legislation. They try, through language, to define what is and is not legal or statutory behavior, either before or after the fact. For lawyers like my father, writing a good contract or law is really about sharply defining the limits of words. When I was a kid, listening to my father talk with his colleagues, or visiting him at the office, I heard so many conversations around definitions. Ordinary words—"gift," "buy," "take," "allow," as well as more complex, Latinate ones —became the exciting subjects of much attention, and seemed to reveal great power and meaning, and also potential danger.

Poets of course are also fascinated with these very same borders, the limits of words. How far can a word be pushed and still mean? Yet not just poets but lawyers too can desire the expansion of the limits of the word, in the interests of permission. I know for my father it could become a deeply satisfying intellectual project, like a serious game, to reimagine the meaning of a phrase, a clause, even a word, to see that it could mean something in a different way, and thus achieve a different result.

And, likewise, poets need in their poems not only to expand but also to define words quite precisely in their contexts, in order to avoid meaningless ambiguity. Poets and lawyers both are deeply concerned with what lies at the limits of language, and the fearful and intensely attractive nothingness beyond.

ONE THING HAS NEVER CHANGED FOR ME ABOUT WRITING PO-etry: I always feel a fear and excitement at the nothingness when I begin. Faced with the emptiness of the page, it can be hard to break the silence, to start saying anything at all. Always in the beginning I have the almost overwhelming feeling that life is too great and too full, too terrifying and too sublime. How could a little poem ever measure up? What will it do that living itself cannot?

But, ultimately, the desire to make something wins out. I begin with very small scratchings, phrases, bits and pieces of something

I can't yet grasp. There is mostly nothing there at the beginning, and I am just trying to make something happen. Maybe just an impulse, or the extremely unformed desire to speak. I try to find the poem by following the language that emerges from somewhere, maybe a personal or collective unconscious, and thinking very hard for a long time about what those words might suggest. There is only the blank page or silence, and the simple desire to speak, to say something that matters.

IT IS THE SILENCE ITSELF THAT DRAWS ME INTO SPEAKING. I feel a silence around each word, a necessary absence that I want to maintain, because I feel to drown out that silence fully, to block it, would be to forget or ignore something I cannot about the reality of our existence. This is, I am sure, why I am a poet, and not a storyteller. For me the silence, that nothingness, always needs to be there.

More than any other use of language, poetry speaks, while also pointing to and reminding us of nothingness. There is an obvious absence at the end of the line, whenever it stops short of the right margin. And look at how the title of a poem just *floats* up there, all alone and ridiculous and forlorn, with white space above and below it. More often than not it's not connected to anything, and there's no structure to support it.

In a poem, we feel what is there, but also what is not. What is not there is brought so close to us that it makes us all the more alive. This is something akin to (but far darker and more dangerous than) the beautiful insufficiency of prayer, the pleasurable ache of being brought as close as possible to the divine, and always falling short.

Poems are, as Federico García Lorca writes, "drawn to the edge of things," and the greatest edge is, of course, our mortality.

This edge of things for Lorca was the line between life and death, what he calls the *duende*. The reason we can find the most powerful energy of *duende* in poetry, even more powerful than in more dramatic forms of art like dance or theater or music, is because of the palpable silence that surrounds a poem.

The silence at the end of a broken line is one of many characteristic visual and aural reminders of the presence of silence. There are the space and silence that surround the title of a poem. The way the title comes out of nowhere, and often doesn't immediately suggest what is coming next, can remind us of how weird language is, and how close to meaninglessness we always are. This effect of the title surrounded by white silence is exacerbated by the leap to the first line of the poem, which again, more often than not, is more obscure and elusive than in other forms of writing.

The form of the poem—its pervasive white spaces, refusals or withdrawals at the ends of lines and between the stanzas—reminds us of nothingness. There is silence too in the leaps of metaphor and symbol and rhyme and association that remind us of gaps in thought, all the ways poetry sometimes behaves like all other forms of writing but can at any moment say "no" to all the usual functions of language, its association and movement as a form of content, the way it refuses to do what it is supposed to do.

WITTGENSTEIN WROTE THAT WHAT WE CANNOT SPEAK ABOUT must be passed over in silence. Or maybe what we cannot speak about can only be conjured in poetry through the mechanism of negation, saying no. This existential negation is only possible when one chooses to write poetry: saying no to all other purposes, to bring us up as close as possible to silence, absence, nothingness, so that we can start to feel what it means to live our lives so close to the abyss. It is, paradoxically, only when we truly start to feel that nothingness, that absence, that the meaning particular to poetry can emerge.

Language leaps, impossibly and essentially, across the inescapable void between name and thing. Words always retain an anarchic, vestigial, latent element of that leap, when at a particular time one person decided to call something *something*, a name. However much we take language for granted in everyday life, in using it we are always close to its provisionality. Nowhere else but in poetry, in both its content and its form, are we made so constantly aware of nothingness, the void.

Through negation, the poet conjures a vacuum into which other possibilities can unexpectedly rush. In so many poems, we see forms of negation: various ways of saying no, not, what is not true, what is not there.

NEGATION CREATES POSSIBILITY. IT ALLOWS ELEMENTS INTO the poem that would not be there if the poet restricted herself to what was real, possible, believed. Through the ordinary mechanism of negation, a spell composed of simple words put into just the right combination is cast in order for us to feel (to use a Freudian term) "uncanny," the emergence of the presence of something strange and unsaid behind what is familiar.

When you look for it, you see negation in poetry everywhere. No, not, can't, won't, all the grammatical forms of saying what is not there, what cannot be, what we will not do. We so often see it at the beginning of poems. The road not taken. Do not go gentle into that good night. My mistress's eyes are nothing like the sun. Allen Ginsberg begins his hilarious, infuriated, sarcastic, tragic poem "America" with a direct address to his subject that is also an assertion of emptiness into which the rest of the poem can flow: "America I've given you all and now I'm nothing."

NEGATION'S FUNCTION IN A POEM MIGHT BE A SIMPLE ONE: TO push away the world and its usual distractions, thereby creating a defined vacuum in perception. Other things then move in, maybe disorganized, but gradually coming to resonate together.

Negation is so often the ultimate statement of a poem: an assertion that is also a withdrawal, a reminder of all that cannot be said. The final negation of a poem thus makes a further thinking and dreaming in the mind of the reader possible. In "The Enigmas" (translated here by Robert Bly), Neruda answers a series of questions from an unnamed you:

> You've asked me what the lobster is weaving there with
> his golden feet?
> I reply, the ocean knows this.
> You say, what is the ascidia waiting for in its transparent
> bell? What is it waiting for?
> I tell you it is waiting for time, like you.

The poem continues with a statement of poetic knowledge, one that relies on negation:

> I am nothing but the empty net which has gone on ahead
> of human eyes, dead in those darknesses,
> of fingers accustomed to the triangle, longitudes
> on the timid globe of an orange.

When the poet says he is himself "nothing," he negates everything he thinks he must be, what the world has told him to do, his responsibilities that come from the outside.

What is left is the imagination, which immediately rushes in to say, in metaphor, that he is, marvelously, "the empty net which has gone on ahead / of human eyes." The human eyes are "dead in those darknesses," they are asleep or blind, and can't see. Fingers have become too accustomed to "the triangle" and "the timid globe of an orange," and can't grasp marvelous things. At the end of the poem, something impossible is caught in the empty net:

> I walked around as you do, investigating
> the endless star,
> and in my net, during the night, I woke up naked,
> the only thing caught, a fish trapped inside the wind.

In the middle of a 1939 elegy for the death of W. B. Yeats, Auden writes emblematically about nothingness and poetry:

> You were silly like us; your gift survived it all:
> The parish of rich women, physical decay,
> Yourself. Mad Ireland hurt you into poetry.
> Now Ireland has her madness and her weather still,
> For poetry makes nothing happen: it survives
> In the valley of its making where executives
> Would never want to tamper, flows on south
> From ranches of isolation and the busy griefs,
> Raw towns that we believe and die in; it survives,
> A way of happening, a mouth.

As so often happens in poetry, a single phrase—poetry makes nothing happen—has been isolated from its context. Depending on your mood, this can be taken to mean that poetry does nothing, a statement of frustration, or maybe a reflection in the poem of the pervasive attitude of executives and revolutionaries that poetry might be more or less nice or cultured, but what is it "for," what does it "do," how does it participate in the great necessities?

But grammatically, in its context, this can also be seen as a statement of what poetry *does*: poetry makes nothing *happen*, that is appear and do and be. The brilliance of this phrase when it is read in the context of the poem is that it simultaneously says and enacts. What it means is what it does. Nothing, a mostly dormant idea that we probably don't think much about (and if so pejoratively), starts to *happen* for us in the poem; that is, become something that we can imagine, think, and wonder about. The "nothing" that poetry makes happen can only happen if the whole poem is considered, and if the movement of the mind from one idea to the next, and so on, is traced and pondered.

In addition to being an elegy for a particular person, the poem is also a reflection of the mood on the eve of World War II. Because "poetry makes nothing happen" it "survives / In the valley of its making." This valley where poetry survives exists because it is made by poetry itself. Perhaps it is retrospective, knowing now what was to come so soon after 1939, but I can't help but hear in these lines a flicker of a fantasy that there would be a valley where something could survive, untouched, whatever calamities were to come.

NEGATION IS CENTRAL NOT ONLY TO POETIC FORM AND SUBJECT, but to the poetic life itself. When I reluctantly tell people I've just met that I am a poet, often they will nervously laugh and ask me how I make a living, as if I spent all day lolling around in the flowers, waiting for a feeling (I wish!). I can see in their eyes the idea that what I do all day is nothing.

I tell my aspiring poetry students that while it turns out that poets are pretty resourceful about making a living, the true occupational hazard is that people will *think* you are lazy, and that you will start to believe them. That doesn't seem like much, but over time it can get quite psychologically debilitating. It's easy, especially when the writing isn't going so well, to feel pretty ridiculous, as if you should have made a different choice with your life, especially when at some point you are home working on a tiny little scrap of a poem for hours while everyone else is at work, making and doing. It's difficult, especially in our culture, to choose to be usefully useless.

There is a story, famous among poets, that the otherwise mostly forgotten French Symbolist poet Saint-Pol-Roux used to attach a sign to his bedroom door before he went to sleep that read "Do not disturb: the poet is working." Poets like this story because it reminds us that our job is, in a way, to refuse to do what others find useful, in order to leave a space for other things to happen.

Poets are alchemists of nothingness. They aspire to turn silence, nothingness, absence, into something palpable. To do so, they must first engage in some ritual of refusal. Only through some turning away, be it extreme or small and temporary (closing the door, shutting off the phone and Internet, refusing to respond to e-mails or to do anything usually considered productive at all), does the poet prepare.

Emily Dickinson famously withdrew. As I mentioned earlier, much has been made of her refusal to engage more actively in the world, though contrary to popular belief she did travel in the earlier part of her life, when she also had an active social life, and even attended boarding school away from Amherst for a year. She did not, however, eventually marry or ever have a family of her own, or any definitively provable romantic attachment, though there is much excited speculation in this regard.

Dickinson refused to follow the pattern of domestic life. She also, despite immense outside pressure and great inner torment, refused to participate in the periodic religious revivals that swept through her town, during which her closest friends would profess their intense religiosity, and even speak in tongues. At great personal cost she made a distinction between official or sanctioned expressions of religiosity—what happened in church—and something more private. Her faith came out of a genuine refusal to lie to herself about her own difficulty in feeling the presence of God. "The Soul's Superior instants / Occur to Her—alone—"

By the end of her life she understood completely the immense importance, not just in religiosity, but in all of life, of what is not said and what is left out.

> By homely gifts and hindered Words
> the human heart is told
> Of Nothing—
> "Nothing" is the force
> That renovates the World—

Dickinson knows the world is too full, which has made it tired, and the human heart is tired too. It and we are in need of renovation. This feels familiar to me. I feel constantly surrounded by too many things, things I have bought or need to buy or am being told are exciting or entertaining. It's exhausting, really. My wife is wise in this way: when it is her birthday she always asks for no presents, just homemade cards. It is the imperfection of these homely gifts and hindered words, the way that they fall short of perfection, that somehow instructs the human heart.

It is the "hindered" words that are not said, or perhaps the words that are said with something hidden or unsaid or held back, that tell us "Of Nothing," the "Nothing" that we need to renovate the world. The words are spoken, and there is still something powerful and unsaid, something to be discovered, a feeling so strong it may not even be possible to put it into words. This feeling can only be truly brought closer to us by a hesitant approximation.

WHITMAN, LIKE DICKINSON, NEVER MARRIED—PROBABLY BE-cause he was clearly attracted mostly or even exclusively to men, though there is at least as much speculation as evidence in this regard. In the form of his poems, as in his life, he was the exact opposite of Dickinson: an extrovert, an inveterate self-promoter, socializer, garrulous and public. For him publication was not the auction of his mind. He wanted fortune and fame and, rare for a poet, got both.

Yet in his poems he too said no and refused in order to say a greater "yes." The first poem of his lifework, *Leaves of Grass*, begins with a great refusal to participate in the ordinary activities of the world: "I loafe and invite my soul, / I lean and loafe at my ease. . . . observing a spear of summer grass." That is the job of the poet, to "loafe," that is, to embody that contradiction of being productively idle. Everything that happens afterward in this poem and the book depends upon that refusal. Civilization tempts him:

> Houses and roof perfumes. . . . the shelves are crowded with
>   perfumes,
> I breathe the fragrance myself, and know it and like it,
> The distillation would intoxicate me also, but I shall not let it.

He "shall not let it"—that is, the lures of the world, the intoxication—distract him from his loafing, the refusal to be tempted out of idleness, from which all his great poetry emerges.

This refusal can be difficult to sustain, because of external and internal pressures. Yet it is only through preserving somewhere, within oneself, a refusal to be "useful" in the ways the world expects, to be "functional" or "productive" or "responsible," that

one prepares to be a poet. The end of Allen Ginsberg's aforemen-
tioned "America" is a refusal to work in order to assert a greater
purpose, hopeful and oblique:

> I'd better get right down to the job.
> It's true I don't want to join the Army or turn lathes
>   in precision parts factories, I'm nearsighted and
>   psychopathic anyway.
> America I'm putting my queer shoulder to the wheel.

Tomaž Šalamun writes, in "Responsibility,"

> who did God consult
> when he made the butterfly as it is
> when he could have made its legs six inches thick
> responsibility responsibility
> baroque sustenance of the people

And this refusal, in the world, to be anything other than a poet
in order to be a poet, can come at great personal cost. Joseph Brod-
sky was hauled before a Soviet court in 1964, when he was twenty-
four years old, charged with "social parasitism"; that is, living off
of the work of others, not having a job. The trial transcript is like
a horribly exaggerated nightmare, funny at times, but mostly de-
pressing. With great dignity Brodsky continually asserts his use-
ful usefulness. "I did work," he says to the judge. "I was writing
poems." And when asked who gave him the right to call himself a
poet, he answered, "No one."

NOT TOO LONG AGO, I WAS GOING THROUGH SOME OLD E-MAILS,
looking for ones that mentioned Tomaž Šalamun, the poet who
had so troubled my father at that reading. Tomaž had recently
died, of lung cancer. My friends and I revered and adored Tomaž,

and I was looking for some correspondence from when we had first met him, to remember those times.

Doing so, I came across an e-mail from my father, written in July 2005, during a brief and misleading respite from the inexorable progression of his tumor. In it, he is writing me about *Profane Halo*, a book of poems by Gillian Conoley that I had left lying around the house on one of my frequent visits home.

I don't know why he picked up that particular book, but coincidentally (or perhaps not), the entire book is haunted by the death of the poet's father. The central poem in the book, in fact, is called "Fatherless Afternoon." There are lots of poems about deaths of fathers, and it's rare to come across one like "Fatherless Afternoon" that honestly, gorgeously, and with true sadness that does not contain an iota of self-pity struggles in a new way with and against the silence of such a devastating pervasive loss. The title of the poem itself already conjures an absence. The poem speaks to the impossibility of fully capturing that absence, and also the need to try.

"Fatherless Afternoon" seems to take place sometime after the initial shock of the death and the funeral, in the time of grieving that is no longer public. In this afternoon of intense private grieving she sees an empty "gray suit in the shape of the drapes there," like a ghost of her father, and the "Blank window at rest now dusty in its corners, no one calling." It's a mysterious, impressionistic poem, full of contradiction, of the pain of absence but also the joy of perception. After remembering her father's suit, and his big gold watch and chain, she looks out the window again:

> Dingy pool of sunlight
> the white mule drinking there
>
> Lucky stag in a waterfall

lucky stag

washing perfume from your moonlit shirts
Tide brings the one who loves you

Tide pulling the world

The ordinary mule gets transformed, in the imagination of
the poet, into a magical animal, a stag. Her father's shirts smell
of perfume. There is an inexorable force, a tide (which also, be-
cause this particular poet can't help but make a joke, is Tide, the
detergent) that pulls the ones we love toward us. The light of the
moon is in the shirts, and also pulls the tides. The father is gone,
and that absence, its vacuum, creates a kind of awareness of the
many marvelous things to see and think about, for those of us who
remain.

I don't know if my father had been reading that poem or an-
other when he wrote me the note below:

> Dearest Matthew: I was wondering whether the poetry I am
> reading is coming out more or less on the same plane to me.
> This one, Profane Halo, was a description of hanging around
> in a place and bumping into people. It sounds like a nice train
> car leading to a house in the Hamptons or Martha's Vineyard
> with hunters, young girls, friends and lovers, etc. This
> reminded me of your second. Am I hooked and unable to grow
> or just enjoying myself. Love, Dad.

More or less on the same plane . . . as what? As me, his son? Or
something the poet meant to say? Some stable meaning that is out
there? I wish I could ask him. Reading this e-mail again just now
I noticed the coincidental echo of "same plane" with the "plain
level" in John Ashbery's "Paradoxes and Oxymorons."

This poem is concerned with language on a very plain level.
Look at it talking to you. You look out a window
Or pretend to fidget. You have it but you don't have it.
You miss it, it misses you. You miss each other.

The book he is reading reminds him of my "second," by which I think he means my second book of poems, which, when I look at the date of the e-mail, I see actually had not been published yet. Though I do not remember doing so, I must have sent him the manuscript at some point. It never until this moment occurred to me the time and effort my father must have put into understanding me, and who I was becoming, without me knowing.

I have read the last sentence of that e-mail innumerable times since finding it again (I have no recollection of first getting it). "Am I hooked and unable to grow or just enjoying myself." I'm not sure exactly what he means. For him it feels like a choice, something he has to decide. Enjoying himself doesn't seem to be compatible with growing, or maybe just not compatible with reading poetry. It could be he is not talking about poetry, but about what it is like to be in this very confusing, completely terrifying, yet somehow still beautiful moment in his life.

Even close to death my father could still find joy, in his family and in his friends, as well as in the small things like good food or company or going out on the water in a boat. His sunny disposition might have been willed at times, but there is also a great wisdom to living that way. Reading these poems might have made him think for a moment of this contradiction, of being at the end, terribly, and somehow also in some strange way enjoying himself.

THE NIGHT MY FATHER DIED, MY MOTHER, BROTHER, SISTER, and I had sat all day with him, in a surreal vigil, in the back room of our house. Though he had been mostly unconscious for days, we talked to him, and to each other, and many hours somehow passed while he labored on. The hospice people had told us that at some point the four of us would have to leave, because he would not die when we were in the room. This seemed impossible, he was so far gone, how could he know? Yet finally, in the very early hours of the next day, without really discussing it we left him alone with a nurse, and went into another part of the house. Just a few minutes later she came rushing into where we were, and told us we should come back, he was going. By the time we got in we were just in time to hear one last breath, maybe a final cough, or just the already abandoned body letting go of one last posthumous exhalation.

We all know when it's time to go; we each will have to cross over alone, into whatever new place or oblivion we believe is there. Each of us will at that moment be, as Stevens says of the listener who listens in the snow, one who "nothing himself, beholds / Nothing that is not there and the nothing that is."

But not yet. For the time being, may it be a long time, we can be together in various ways. My favorite poem of all is one of the very last written by the lawyer, Stevens, "Final Soliloquy of the Interior Paramour." I believe this interior paramour has a hidden desire to be together with others, to somehow share with other people the very private act of imagining:

> Light the first light of evening, as in a room
> In which we rest and, for small reason, think
> The world imagined is the ultimate good.

> This is, therefore, the intensest rendezvous.
> It is in that thought that we collect ourselves,
> Out of all the indifferences, into one thing:

Within a single thing, a single shawl
Wrapped tightly round us, since we are poor, a warmth,
A light, a power, the miraculous influence.

Here, now, we forget each other and ourselves.
We feel the obscurity of an order, a whole,
A knowledge, that which arranged the rendezvous.

Within its vital boundary, in the mind.
We say God and the imagination are one . . .
How high that highest candle lights the dark.

Out of this same light, out of the central mind,
We make a dwelling in the evening air,
In which being there together is enough.

The scene is a group of people, in the evening. A presence is felt, powerful and benevolent, as together they create a kind of secular holy space, dedicated to the imagination. They are reading together, and in doing so, they are pushing something away, and also bringing something into being, a space. This space is created by an act, once again of negation, this time of forgetting "each other and ourselves." It is only then that another consciousness can begin to emerge.

Immediately upon forgetting themselves, the people begin in the room to "feel the obscurity of an order, a whole / A knowledge, that which arranged the rendezvous." They start not only to feel, but to know, something about this greater order, a "knowledge," that which put them together in this place. This seems to me to be very close to a religious experience. When people ask me if I am a religious person, I say no because I don't go to houses of worship or engage regularly in formal rituals. But, because of poetry, I silently think yes.

This knowledge has a "vital boundary, in the mind." The mind is where the poem happens. In ordinary usage the word "vital" most often is a synonym for important, or essential, but its origin is the Latin word for life, "*vita*." This moment of feeling the "world imagined" is intimately connected with the basic fact of being alive. And, it is connected with the feeling of a boundary, beyond which there is that old nothingness.

The last lines of the poem remind me of the comfort I have felt in small gatherings, in difficult moments. And as well of certain times when I have been in the audience listening to poetry, and have in the faces of my fellow strangers noticed, and myself felt, a kind of relaxed, wistful, dreamy attention, not necessarily even toward a particular poem, but toward possibility.

In this paradoxically collective yet also private space, something extraordinary can happen. "Out of this same light, out of the central mind, / We make a dwelling in the evening air, / In which being there together is enough," despite our knowledge of all the terrible things, and the ultimate nothingness that surrounds and awaits us. Poetry isn't a consolation for death, nothingness, the void. It's possible poetry only sharpens that painful knowledge. But being there together, alone and with others, in a place of great generous attention, is and is not enough, we say, grateful for the light, aware of the dark.

afterword

Poetry and Poets in a Time of Crisis

FOR A LONG TIME NOW, SINCE AT LEAST THE ARRIVAL OF THE new millennium, it has been clear to many of us that we are coming to a crisis, if we have not already arrived. A destabilized future yawns before us as a great, worrisome vacuum into which all our most terrifying visions can easily rush. At one point, we might have thought we had some idea about the shape of the future, its challenges and structures, but it seems we do not. Maybe we did not all along.

I am a poet, which means that my areas of expertise and concern are language and the imagination. I feel certain it is essential to ask, what does this crisis mean for poets, and poetry? What, in these times, must we do? Can poetry help save us?

I have always believed that poetry has its own special role, distinct from all other uses of language. I agree with W. S. Merwin when he writes, "Poetry like speech itself is made out of paradox, contradictions, irresolvables. . . . It cannot be conscripted even into the service of good intentions." He then goes on to explain, however, that circumstances can challenge this belief:

> *Poets have been known to be smug about their fine uselessness, but the Vietnam War led many poets of my generation to try to use poetry to make something stop happening. We will never know whether all that we wrote shortened that nightmare by one hour, saved a single life or the leaves on one tree, but it seemed unthinkable to many of us not to make the attempt and not to use whatever talent we had in order to do it. In the process we produced a great many bad poems, but our opposition to that horror and degradation was more than an intellectual formulation, and sometimes it tapped depths of bewilderment, grief, rage, admiration, that took us by surprise. Occasionally it called for writings that may be poems after all.*

It may very well be that we have entered another time when most poets will feel compelled to use poetry to stop things from happening. Yet I believe that even if poetry did not do this, it would be vital to our survival.

It has always seemed to me that if you want to convince someone to act in a certain way, or to explain why something is right and something else is wrong, prose is far better than poetry. Poems of course at times convince, explain, advocate, argue, but in the end, they always are ultimately interested in something else. We could call that something else beauty, or the possibilities of language, or maybe just freedom. It is something that has to do with allowing the mind to be completely, almost anarchically interested in the freedom to explore the possibilities of the material of language itself.

That is what makes poems an undependable vehicle for advocacy. The poem is easily distracted. It wanders away from the demonstration, the committee meeting, the courtroom, toward the lake or that intriguing, mysterious light over there. What is that light? It looks like something, I'm not sure what, I'm sorry to leave this very important conversation but I have to know.

This wandering, though, is not a mere luxury or privilege. It has an essential purpose. In Wallace Stevens's essay "The Noble Rider and the Sound of Words," he makes the argument that poetry is a place where we can preserve our imaginations, and resist the "pressure of the real," that is, the incessant drumming in of information, of news, of terrible events and realities. If we do not do so, he argues, we lose something essential to our humanity: our imagination.

Stevens wrote his essay on the eve of the entry of the United States into World War II, when the news was pressing down on everyone. The drumming of information he was identifying has become immeasurably louder. Sometimes I feel like I can't hear anything else. Sometimes it seems to me that unless I turn off all the electronics in my immediate vicinity, I will be surrounded by a kind of existential buzzing, a deafening sound composed of everyone's thoughts, opinions, commentaries, clever jokes, contradictory certainties, intense worries, gateless fears.

That all this loudness takes place in language seemed to be of special concern to me as a poet, since my artistic work depends on freedom and lightness but also serious attention to that same language. To be continually surrounded by language used exclusively for utilitarian purposes is a threat to the disinterested yet sacred attention a poet must have to words. Also, poetry has an intimate, necessary relation with silence. The work of poets is impaired by too much noise and language, a scarcity of silence.

This communication has over time become not only intolerable to me personally, but also a matter of immediate, wider concern. The pressure of the real is everywhere. It's completely understandable grief, and fear, and freaking out. And also community, and necessary information. Some find solace on social media and elsewhere, that really does make sense. Networks will surely be a source of action and resistance. We need to know what's happening.

But there is a point where it becomes too much, a kind of roar of opinions and fears that do not truly stir us to action or make us more aware. There is a danger to unfettered catastrophizing, which will sap our energy and distract and drain us. On social media and elsewhere, our attention has been monetized, not figuratively but literally, to a personally and societally harmful degree.

When Stevens discusses the pressure of the real, he talks about it as a violence done to our very selves. He writes that poetry is the way we can resist that pressure, that violence, not in order to avoid the real, but in order to preserve within ourselves the necessary space of imagination, possibility, humanity, love, a space that can help us live our lives. Poetry, because it is ultimately undistracted by whatever uses to which language is otherwise devoted (telling stories, arguing or convincing or informing, buying and selling, preaching, condemning, and so on) has a unique role in this preservation of an imaginative space.

I am sure that what we need is to work on cultivating within ourselves a condition of vigilant, clear-eyed readiness. We do not know what is to come. Whatever it is, we will need to act, to resist, and not to sink into passive acceptance, if it turns out what happens is not as bad as our worst fears. We cannot allow ourselves to already be so tired out by battling our own phantasms that we cannot act when it is time.

Poets, if you find yourselves worrying that your poems are not "about" political matters, here is my suggestion: every single time you feel that worry, finish your poem, make it as beautiful as you can, and then do some kind of concrete action. Regardless of how poets feel about aesthetic matters, we all agree we are citizens. We have the same obligations to activism and engagement as anyone else.

Some poets I know have been working very hard in these ways for a long time. Others of us have been mostly asleep. One of the only good things I can say about this undeniable crisis is that it has made absolutely clear what some have never forgotten: that we all need to wake up and start putting our queer shoulders to the wheel (Ginsberg, "America"). Whatever kind of poetry anyone writes, or whatever art we make, there is always time to do the necessary work of making our society better.

There is another reason why a resistance to the pressure of the real, and the preservation of a free imaginative space in language, is vital to our survival. In some ways it seems to me that the greatest of all the problems we face as a species is our inability to understand each other. This happens in individual relations of course, but more troublingly, there are obvious and growing divides among entire groups who see the world in radically different ways. Often it seems as if these groups are living in several separate worlds (blue and red America, secular and fundamentalist, rich and poor, black and white, and so on, overlappingly), each with their own facts. Maybe it has always been this way, and it is only now with pervasive instantaneous modes of communication that we realize this.

What is the special role of poetry in this condition? Poets, according to Stevens, help us live our lives, not by telling us what to think, or by comforting us. They do so by creating spaces where one individual imagination can activate another, and those imaginations can be together. Poems are imaginative structures built out of words, ones that any reader can enter. They are places of freedom, enlivenment, true communion.

One could say, correctly, that this is true of any form of literature, or really any use of language. But because poetry remains free of all the other obligations that any other use of language inevitably must take on, it can be devoted purely to the creation of these spaces, where one imagination in the company of another can remember what it is to be alive and free.

The creation of these imaginative spaces is necessary work. It seems to me that widespread refusal to acknowledge obvious truths about the problems that face us is not due to ignorance or lack of information. It is not that people have not been told enough times what our problems are, and what we need to do about them. People do not disbelieve in inequality or racism or global warming because they have not been informed: they disbelieve because they cannot or choose not to imagine. They are cruel because to them, others have become an abstraction, and cannot be truly imagined.

People who do not have irreparably psychologically damaged minds can be healed. They can change. This is not the work of information, but of the imagination. As impossible as it might seem, it may be that true poetry is the only way we can begin to see each other again.

The role of poetry in our time of crisis is the same as always: to preserve our minds and language, so we may be strong for whatever is to come. And also, to preserve the possibility of mutual understanding, not by arguing for it, but by demonstrating it.

Two days after the 2016 presidential election, I taught my graduate seminar in poetry, which meets Thursday nights. On the one hand, it seemed ludicrous to blithely continue moving through the syllabus without acknowledging what the students were feeling. On the other, for days, my students and colleagues had been talking of nothing but their shock and fear and confusion. The atmosphere was already heightened to an almost impossible degree, so devoting several hours to talking about what we were already all only talking and thinking about felt intolerable.

The only thing I could think of to do was to ask everyone to bring in poems that they loved, so that we could read them aloud, and just sit and listen. Sitting and listening to poetry for an hour or so was not some kind of cure. For some, it didn't really even seem to help. Some students cried, others seemed not to be very present. Their bodies were in the room but their minds were still wandering through anxious, uncertain, shifting futures.

I ended class by reading one of my favorite poems, by Frank O'Hara, "A True Account of Talking to the Sun at Fire Island." In the poem, the sun comes to O'Hara early in the morning. The sun first reproaches the poet for not being awake when he comes, and then gives him some encouragement, with a bad pun on his first name: "Frankly, I wanted to tell you / I like your poetry. I see a lot / on my rounds and you're ok. You may not be / the greatest thing on earth, but / you're different." The class full of aspiring poets laughed.

The sun goes on to tell the poet he should look up more often, and to "always embrace things, people earth / sky stars, as I do, freely and with / the appropriate sense of space." I almost never cry, but I got choked up, just as I do every single time I read this poem, because even though O'Hara died at the age of forty, after being hit by a Jeep on the beach at Fire Island, a year before I was born, I love him, and am sure I know him.

The poem ends:

"Sun, don't go!" I was awake
at last. "No, go I must, they're calling
me."
        "Who are they?"
                Rising he said "Some
day you'll know. They're calling to you
too." Darkly he rose, and then I slept.

They are calling to you too, in poems. Some day you'll know. This is the promise of poetry, in this time of crisis, and beyond.

acknowledgments

SO MUCH OF THIS BOOK WAS WRITTEN AS A RESULT OF CONVER-
sations I had over many years with so many different people,
friends and strangers. I am sure that I will never be able to com-
pletely and adequately thank all those whom I should. I thank first
of all those who took the time to share with me their feelings about
poetry, what they do and do not understand, and why. Those con-
versations were essential to me.

Many people read previous versions of this book, or had
sustained conversations with me about various aspects of it,
for which I am so grateful: Travis Nichols, Deborah Landau,
Srikanth Reddy, Rob Casper, Catherine Barnett, Lisa Olstein,
Daniel Handler, Meghan O'Rourke, Ava Sakaya Rosen, Jen Hyde,
Libby Edelson, Steve Almond, Ben Herman, Alexandra Zapruder,
Michael Zapruder, Caroline Paul, Constance Hale, Melanie
Gideon, Diana Kapp, Natalie Baszile, Jill Bialosky, Jae Choi,

Charlie D'Ambrosio, David Kermani, Charlie Wright, Joshua Beckman, Matt Rohrer, Anthony McCann, Douglas Crase, Rodney Koenecke, Ellen Welcker, Robin Rinaldi, Rob Winger, Kerri Arsenault, Tod Goldberg, David Ulin, Brett Lauer, Missy Mazzoli, Gabriel Kahane, Ann Hood, Kevin Young, Nick Flynn, Lacy M. Johnson, Brenda Hillman, Robert Hass, Eula Biss, Emily Rapp, Lynne Bermont, and Ilya Kaminsky.

I also thank the Tin House Summer Writer's Workshop, and especially Lance Cleland and Cheston Knapp: the writing of this book began with a lecture I gave there many years ago. Thank you to the Academy of American Poets, for asking me to write about W. S. Merwin, and to David Ulin, for whom I wrote an essay about form and rhyme that turned into one of the chapters. I thank my colleagues at the San Francisco Writers' Grotto, the MFA at UCR Palm Desert, at Saint Mary's College of California, and other places where I was fortunate to write and to teach. I am grateful as well for the support of the Guggenheim Foundation and the Lannan Foundation.

I owe an especial debt to my poetry teachers: Dara Wier, as well as the late James Tate and the late Agha Shahid Ali. I also want to express my gratitude to all the wonderful students I have had over the years. It was with you that I refined so many of the ideas that appear in this book, and it has been a great pleasure and honor to have worked with all of you.

Thank you to Bill Clegg, who continues to show so much faith in me and my work. Thank you to the great Dan Halpern and Ecco Press, who long before I met them published so many books that taught me so much, and now have given me the opportunity to publish this one. I want especially to thank the immensely patient and perceptive Gabriella Doob, who edited this book in so many different versions, with unfailing good spirits. I could not have written this book without her. Thank you as well to Michael Taeckens and Fred Courtright. And, with especial love, I thank Michael Wiegers and Joseph Bednarik and Kelly Forsythe and the rest of my family at Copper Canyon Press, for taking such good care of my poems, and therefore of me.

Finally, of course, there is my beloved and brilliant wife, Sarah, who has been so patient and supportive all these years, and my precious son, Simon. I love you both, you are my life and my great joy.

credits

index

about the author

Matthew Zapruder is the author of four collections of poetry. His poetry, essays, and translations have appeared in publications including *The New Yorker*, *The Paris Review*, *Tin House*, and *The Believer*. An associate professor in the Saint Mary's College of California MFA program and English department, he is also editor at large at Wave Books and, from 2016 to 2017, was the editor of the poetry page of the *New York Times Magazine*. He lives in Oakland, California, with his wife and son.